# Tillers of the August Moon

The Untold Story and History of the Satellite
That Revolves Around Planet Earth

by
Michael E. Morgan

# Tillers of the August Moon

The Untold Story and History of the Satellite Revolving Around the Earth

Copyright © 2025 by Michael E. Morgan

All rights reserved. No part of this book may be reproduced or transmitted in any form or by any means now known or to be invented, electronic or mechanical, including photocopying, recording, or by any information storage and retrieval system without written permission from the author or publisher, except for the inclusion of brief quotations in a review.

For information write to:
Dawntrader Books, LLC
P.O.Box D120-413
Scottsdale, Arizona
85266

If you are unable to order this book from your local bookseller, or Amazon.com, you may order directly from the publisher.
Quantity discounts for organizations are available.

Cover and book design by
Michael E. Morgan

Publisher's Cataloging-in-Publication Data
ISBN 9-798992-7032-1-4

10 9 8 7 6 5 4 3 2 1

Table of Contents

Preface..................................................................................4

Introduction ........................................................................14

Chapter 1. Lions, Reptilians and UFOs, Oh My............................... 24
Chapter 2. The Chi Ahkar Gambit..........................................36
Chapter 3. Mining at the Base camp........................................48
Chapter 4. Trouble From the Home World............................... 60
Chapter 5. Who Goes There....................................................67
Chapter 6. Assault on the Lunar Station..................................73
Chapter 7. Holographic Transmitters, Mind Control..............78
Chapter 8. Friends or Enemies............................................... 82
Chapter 9. Disclosure Myth, Dark Agenda..............................90
Chapter 10. Secret Deals to be Made.....................................101
Chapter 11. The Soul Collector Vortex .................................109
Chapter 12. Reincarnation Hack, The Soul Trap...................130
Chapter 13. The Abduction Zone.......................................... 138
Chapter 14. Implants, Alien Tracers..................................... 142
Chapter 15. The Secret Space program.................................146
Chapter 16 God vs Evolution... ............................................184
Chapter 17. The Galactic Federation of Worlds.................... 190
Chapter 18. The Cleansing, Earth in Upheaval.....................204
Chapter 19. Ascension, Not Staying the Same......................213
Chapter 20. The Time Loop Matrix...................................... 227
Chapter 21. Tribulation, Precursor to ascension...................235
Chapter 22. Crop Circles, Alien Tracers............................... 251
Chapter 23. Level One Civilization.......................................257
Chapter 24. Quantum, The Multiverse Hive Mind................274
Chapter 25. Sentient A.I., Alien Slave Master...................... 282
Chapter 26. Alchemy of the Soul..........................................293

Epilogue..............................................................................302

## Preface

It is the year 1969. The United States is ready to launch the first successful lunar rocket, the Saturn 5. This feat of engineering fell on the heels of many disastrous attempts to create rockets powerful enough to reach space.

The negotiations at the Yalta conference toward the end of WWII, involving Franklin Roosevelt, Joseph Stalin and Winston Churchill, discussed the progress of the war in Europe and the potential for the allied efforts to end the war with Japan. The treatise between the US and Russia fell apart when Roosevelt died. The technological spoils after the fall of Germany, then were divided between Russia and the US.

Werner Von Braun and other German scientists were given immunity from war crimes and brought to the United States under Operation Paperclip after the end of the war. Operation Paperclip was a secret United States intelligence program in which more than 1,600 German scientists, engineers, and technicians were taken from former Nazi Germany to the U.S. for government employment between 1945–1959 with NASA.

The U.S. Joint Chiefs of Staff officially

## Preface

established Operation Overcast on July 20, 1945, with the dual aim of leveraging German expertise to assist in the ongoing war effort against Japan, and to bolster U.S. postwar military research. The US then began using German V2 rockets for atmospheric research and explored the ballistic capability of these rockets later. The United States formed the National Aeronautics and Space Agency in 1958, to further the applications of the peaceful use of space. In the 1950s, a variety of medium and long-range missiles were developed and became the starting point of the US space program. Missiles like Redstone, Atlas and Titan would eventually launch astronauts into space.

Then the race to space between the United States and Russia was marked by the Soviet launching of Sputnik 1, the first orbiting satellite in in 1957. This development was a shock to the US. The satellite was designed by Russia to conquer space for military purposes and prove military supremacy between the two nations.

Then the US followed with America's first satellite in January 1958, with the Jet Propulsion Laboratory launch of Explorer 1. Then Russia launched the Russian Luna 1 probe to the moon in 1959. Their successful launch of Luna 1 saw the rocket fly past the moon. Later, America launches the first weather satellite in February of that year, with The Vanguard 2 satellite used to forecast the weather. In 1961, Russia looms ahead again with the first man in orbit around the earth with Yuri Gagarin as the first astronaut.

Then America casts its bid next with their first astronaut, John Glenn, to orbit the earth in 1962 while they also launched the first two interplanetary Mariner probes to Venus in July. At that time, the US began the Ranger series of nine probes to the moon from 1961 to 1966 to take photos of the lunar surface in preparation for a lunar landing.

The desperation to catch up with an even bolder move against its rival, to advance man's lofty aspirations of developing the future of space exploration is when President Kennedy announced in 1962, a determined demand to put a man on the moon by 1969.

The Saturn 5 rocket sat on the launch pad at Cape Canaveral poised to launch a three-man crew to the moon. Man's first attempt to land a manned

Preface

crew to set down on the lunar surface would surely redefine the United States once again as the supreme power on earth by capturing and securing the first military base on the moon.

The United States would learn of a great secret, the first of many secrets about our lunar neighbor which would shatter any previous ideas regarding our romantic notion with this august body.

In 1969, the first lunar lander, part of the Apollo program, sat down successfully in tranquility crater. Neal Armstrong would make his historic statement about setting foot on the lunar surface. During January 31st to February 9th,1971. The Apollo 14 mission launched with Alan Shepard, Command Module Pilot Stuart Roosa and Lunar Module Pilot Edgar Mitchell to again return to the moon. While Shepard and Mitchell were on the surface, Roosa remained in Lunar orbit aboard the Command and Service Module, performing scientific experiments and photographing the Moon, including the landing site of the future Apollo 16 mission. It was the eighth crewed mission in the United States Apollo Program, the third to Land on the Moon, and the first to land in the Lunar highlands. It was the last of the "H missions", landings at specific sites of scientific interest on the Moon for two-day stays with two lunar Extravehicular activities (EVAs or moonwalks).

The primary objectives of these missions were to explore the Fra Mauro region centered around deployment of the Apollo Lunar Surface Scientific Experiments Package, or ALSEP; lunar field geology investigations; collection of surface material samples for return to Earth; deployment of other scientific instruments not part of ALSEP; orbital science involving high-resolution photography of future candidate landing sites; photography of deep-space phenomena, such as zodiacal light and gegenschein (a faint light about 20 degrees across on the celestial sphere opposite the sun, probably caused by backscatter of sunlight by solar-system dust); communications tests using S-band and VHF signals to determine reflective properties of the lunar surface; engineering and operational evaluation of hardware and techniques; tests to determine variations in S-band signals; and the photography of surface details from 60 nautical

## Preface

miles in altitude.

Mitchell was the first astronaut to notice that they were not alone in this adventure. Utilizing a previously agreed upon code with Houston, the astronauts were told that if they were to encounter any alien craft (UFO) on the moon, they would refer to them as 'Santa Claus', a code name on a private communicating channel, thus keeping this amazing discovery from public knowledge.

Even though Nasa was using a very high frequency for this private channel with Houston, many shortwave radio operators on earth were able to tune in to this private channel. The Ham radio operators heard Edgar commenting after exiting the lander, Santa Claus was watching them from the rim of the crater.

Then, the next surprise mystery arose when the astronauts completed part of their mission to plant several seismic sensors on the surface, set to record the impact of the lunar lander escape booster falling back to the surface from a planned altitude, while the escape module rejoined the orbiting return vehicle.

When the escape booster struck the lunar surface,

its purpose was to measure the thickness and perhaps nature of the interior of the moon through the vibration of the impact. This experiment meant to derive some clue regarding the material of the moon and perhaps to determine it might reveal if the moon was made of the same material as the earth. Upon impact however, Houston was stunned to learn after the seismic monitors recorded the vibration, the vibration continued for more than an hour, indicating that the moon might have cave-like structures, because it rang like a bell.

Then on the next lunar mission, a similar experiment conducted with a heavier booster falling from a greater altitude caused the ringing again, but this time it rang for more than eight hours. This confirmed that the interior was not a pocket, as was the supposed cave-like anomaly, but that the entire lunar interior might be hollow.

This remarkable data brought a revisiting of previous analyses about other lunar anomalies that were previously ignored. First, that the earth's gravitational field was not strong enough to hold a moon of this size into a sustainable orbit about the earth. Second, that the orbit around the earth was a near precise circle, also thought to be curious, as no other known moon orbits this way, normally elliptical not circular. Third, That the rotation of the moon is in complete tidal lock, meaning that a view from the earth would never reveal the back side of the moon. The fourth and final oddity, the size of the moon's diameter and distance from the earth provided perfect eclipses with the sun, also quite curious. All these oddities represented together, an absolute mathematical improbability with the obvious and inescapable conclusion that the moon was artificial! There have been many theories about the origin of the moon. The fact that Iridium is very rare on earth but plentiful on the moon showed up in the moon rock analysis. The idea that the moon might be from somewhere else was kept from the public.

  Not unlike landers on Mars, the lunar landers have shown to have several objects located on the dark side that defy logical explanation, objects that are not considered natural formations, suggesting someone else's handywork, by their shape and size. Though these exceptions seem to violate the generally excepted rule, these artifacts are still believed publicly to be natural in their essence, though they have been vigorously argued by other independent proponents of scientific evaluation. These artifacts are from an extraterrestrial influence, but opinions from the mainstream proponents simply debunked these ideas and were dismissed by the voices of 'scientific reason.'

These facts represent formidable mysteries that form the basis of this remarkable story. Years after Mitchell returned to earth, he continued to proclaim his belief in UFOs and extraterrestrial entities that do exist. Elements of the CIA disinformation program and through the United States Air Force Project Blue Book, as well as Naval intelligence succeeded to discredit Mitchell and others who have functioned as whistle blowers publicly through their declarations.

Although this story is structured as fiction, it is presented as a what if scenario. Ancient Sumerian historical texts, more than 6,000 years old, detail historical accounts of the 'Gods' (extraterrestrial species) who arrived on earth hundreds of thousands of years ago. These historical documents are treated as mythical fantasies, which may

## Preface

eventually prove to be more like the elements of science fact in the not-so-distant future. In the meantime, a warning is warranted. Should you want to read further, unless you are willing for your belief system to be altered permanently, do not read this book!

**Below is an approximate timeline of events in pre history:**

**A.** Sons of 'god'-Prime Mover (Djinn) exist before creation in the quantum.
**B.** 13 billion BCE emergence of Feminine Djinn/ Fall and 3D multiverse begins.
**C.** 4 billion years BCE, Lyran progenitors seed Tiamat in 5th orbit/3.5 billion BCE is destroyed by Nibiru, leaving asteroid belt and remainder becomes Earth in 3rd orbit.
**D.** 1 billion BCE Tiamat rebuilt with second seeding and creation of artificial moon and black knight satellite.
**E.** 1.5 million BCE fallen take on Simian hosts evolve between water vs land development.
**F.** 1 million BCE 4th infusion of fallen successful.
**G.** 750,000 BCE Lemurian/Atlantean culture evolution/rogue moon enters orbit around earth.
**H.** 450,000 BCE Anunnaki arrive from Nibiru to mine gold.
**I.** 425,000 BCE Anunnaki create homo Sapien from Homo Erectus to mine gold.
**J.** 400,000 BCE Atlantean – Lemurian wars.
**K.** 239,000 BCE Second moon falls out of orbit and destroys Lemuria.
**L.** Watchers marry adomite women and give birth to nephilum
**M.** 179,000 BCE Atlantean empire begins.
**N.** 59,000 BCE Anunnaki royals leave earth with 9 generals left behind to rule. .
**O.** 50,000 BCE Chi Ahkar Draco invasion of earth and moon takeover.
**P.** 45,000 BCE Marduk and Yahweh engage in nuclear war in the Mesopotamian valley.
**Q.** 12,886 BCE Dryas - Flood Gigemesh (Noah) survives.
**R** 8,000-6,000 BCE Pre - Sumerian civilization.
**S.** 5,000 BCE Pre-Ahkken -Mesopotamian empire.
**T.** 4,500-530 BCE kingdoms of Iraq-Israel.

Approximately 5 billion years ago, a progenitor race of feline humanoids chose a large planet in the Milky Way galaxy to seed with life biologics which they called Tiamat, existing in the fifth orbit within the main sequence star Sol near the rim of the galaxy.

There were several progenitor races charged by Source, the prime mover, with the task of spreading life about the galaxy. They had conducted surveys of several star systems in this quadrant, but they were very optimistic about this system because they always favored young sequence stars over older more mature solar bodies for their stability and youthful promise of a long and fruitful support for the evolution of a third density world.

They had completed their mission and about to return to their home world Lyra, a fifth density world enjoying a level 7 technological development. Their peaceful existence was well known in the third density of the universe until they were betrayed by the aggressive behavior of the Chi Ahkar empire of Draco reptilians from Orion.

That confrontation eventually erupted into several major conflicts, known as the Lyran-Orion wars. Those wars lasted for millennia. Unfortunately, many Lyran died during those conflicts because the Chi Ahkar were more advanced technologically at the time. The Lyrans were out matched by the Draco reptilians as they were fierce warriors in battle.

The Draco reptilians were humanoids, large in stature, standing over 10 feet in height. Their bodies bore a strong muscular and powerful build. Their hands were webbed with sharp claws and their feet also webbed. They sported tails that dropped sharply to the ground behind them which helped in their balance with swift movements. They could swing them around defensively, moving smartly with tremendous agility. Their fighting style was brutally fierce carrying laser pulse weapons as pistols and rifles as well as short swords as additional side armament.

The adult males had bat-like wings that folded into the upper spine enabling them to fly short distances making them formidable adversaries. Their eyes bore slitted pupils with a yellowish tint and a double eyelid that limited strong light to enter. The eyes set deeply into the sides of their skulls beneath angular fore brows. They had keen vision at great distances and able to see clearly in near total darkness. Their skin shown all over with greenish to brown thick scales providing them with almost invincible defenses.

On the other hand, the Lyrans were shorter by comparison, not more than 9 feet in height on average. Their heads were distinctly feline with a thick brownish mane and bore large tiger-like fangs and strong jaws. Their bodies were covered with short thick hair and their hands were more like paws with sharp claws but retractable. Their eyes were amber with rounded black pupils having a bluish tint that carried an illuminescent glow in the dark. Their strength lay in a strong and muscular upper torso but with thin very powerful legs, which allowed them to run quickly and able to leap in high vaults and over large distances. They preferred to choose the high ground as part of their offensive strategy.

Psychologically, the Dracos were militaristic and belligerent in nature having little or no respect for life contrasting to the Lyrans who always looked to negotiate differences instead of resorting to

# Introduction

conflict and tending toward a respect for all life. Spiritually very advanced they possessed shape-shifting abilities into higher densities.

At the end of the major conflicts, the Lyran survivors retreated in defeat. Ultimately, the Lyrans sought refuge in the fifth density to escape total annihilation.

Despite a thorough investigation of the Sol system, which included the secondary system of 7 planets encircling the twin dwarf star Aluthe, which followed a long 20,000 year-long elliptical path about the sequence star. Its path tilted at a thirty-degree angle against the plane of the ecliptic, indicating a free and undisturbed passage through the main solar system of 9 planets, which included five denser bodies later to be called, Mercury, Venus, Segulus and Mars inclusive of Tiamat. Then, followed by the outer gas giants later called Jupiter, Saturn, Uranus and Neptune.

During the adjustment period while the solar system was balancing, Segulus was push out of its orbital path by the gas giant Jupiter, leaving the third orbital path empty between Venus and Mars. Segulus, now a rogue planet, continued to sail into interstellar space aiming toward the Andromeda galaxy.

Then a billion years later, the twin dwarf star's path along with its 7 planets shifted closer to Jupiter causing one of the smaller moons of the sixth planet called Rhegol, to enter onto a direct collision course with Tiamat. The impact was catastrophic, shattering Tiamat into thousands of pieces and casting its moon away from the planet leaving one larger chunk which drifted out of the fifth orbit and settled into the third orbit. The remainder of Tiamat and its moon became a belt of asteroids between Mars and Jupiter.

The Lyrans returned to remedy the calamity by gathering thousands of ice comets from the Oort cloud, which extended beyond Neptune at the forming of the solar system. The comets began to impact the remainder of Tiamat until it was almost completely a water world. Then the Lyrans brought the world into a spin, churning its molten metallic core providing a magnetic shield to block harmful cosmic energy from reaching the surface. This geomagnetic sphere allowed a thick atmosphere to collect from the nitrogen and oxygen inside the

## Introduction

comets as well.

With the new planet closer to Sol, some of the liquid water lifted into the growing atmosphere creating a canopy of vapor that would help protect the new seedlings from the intense solar energy impacting the third orbit.

The last task was to provide an artificial replacement moon to provide the necessary tidal lock for a balanced ecological weather system. The Lyrans provided a crew to maintain the hollow moon from within its interior; while reseeding the remnant planet with more complex biologics, this defined the Cambrian explosion which reset the new planet onto a more accelerated evolutionary level.

Finally, an automated satellite was placed in polar orbit (now referred to as the dark knight) to monitor the continued evolutionary progress. Satisfied now that the system was back on track and order restored, they left for their home world. Life developed as expected. The Lyrans looked back on their handywork and commented to each other about what they shall name this new formed world? They paused to consider the question.

"We will call it Earth, they concluded, for it means

'hope for a new beginning' as we have made it a world not unlike our own in its image. Perhaps we will return one day to see what evolution will produce. In the meantime, our crew aboard the moon along with our satellite will help to manage this turbulent but promising system."

The life span of a typical Lyran was almost eternal and Godlike, lasting for millions of years. It would be several hundred-million years before the Chi Ahkar would discover the beauty of Earth lying within the Sol system as a brilliant emerald-blue gem presenting itself with an attractive promise of its natural resources ripe for the taking.

Life was still primitive and presented little or no resistance to their invasion plans. Though the Dracos built a vast colony of worlds in the Mica system, their insatiable greed for more delivered copious amounts of saliva to uncontrollably drip from the horrible grimace of razor-sharp teeth while they peered through their long-range scanners.

There were many worlds to choose from however, the newly organized collective known as the Galactic Federation of Worlds would create certain problems for them should they force their way into restricted regions of many budding new worlds. This would be a considerable inconvenience should they need to engage with the Federation at this time. They were confident in any future conflict with the Federation because they knew that it comprised many star systems that were mere fledglings with lesser developed technology compared to theirs.

Their observations of the earth indicated that other lifeforms came to earth to mine the minerals rich within the soil of the planet. One such species were the Anunnaki, a humanoid race also of reptilian genetics, though austere and intelligent and less militaristic, they were of a royal dynasty and had no particular interest in the indigenous life forms on the planet nor any interest in the claiming or commandeering the earth for their own possession. For them, it was a simple matter of necessity and survival. It was a practical matter that gold was present on earth and did not exist beyond the Kuyper belt of planets. They needed gold in abundant quantities. They sorely needed it to help secure a failing atmosphere on their home world, Nibiru, a large planet that encircled the dwarf star of the Sol system.

In their occupation of earth, they built many colonies during their stay. After 450,000 years, they returned to their home world. Though the royals left a contingent behind to rule the colonies of humanoids, called Adamites, genetically altered to assist in their mining operations, the earth experienced more calamities which dissuaded any desire for a longer stay. The last of their kind left earth around 13,000 BCE.

The Chi Ahkar empire saw their opportunity to swiftly move in and take over the mining operations of the Anunnaki without concerns from any Federation oversight. Soon after their arrival however, the Dracos became aware of an uprising and rebellion in their home world empire in the Mica system. So, they left and with two battalions behind to continue the gold mining operations. It was not long before the battalion commanders realized the armada was not coming back.

They decided to make earth their own world and settled in the vast deep underground tunnels they constructed because surface dwelling was not an option for them due to the intense light and heat from the star Sol. The artificial moon station was a problem which needed to be solved. They began to make plans for an assault on the moon.

Strategically, the moon would become their perfect military high ground to preserve their domination of the planet and all species that lived there. In addition, the satellite would serve as a vanguard for a possible invasion force should the armada return one day.

There are countless extraterrestrial species in the galaxy and that is just the Milky Way. Now with the advent of the Hubble and the James Webb space telescopes we know there are at least billions if not trillions of other galaxies with exoplanets expanding to distances measured by trillions of light years (as the distance light travels at 186,000 miles per second in a year). Can you imagine that? Well, if you can, you are a brighter person than this author. This author has great difficulty embracing those kinds of astronomical numbers. So, the idea that we are the only life form present seems quite absurd really. Then, given how small earth is relative within our own solar system, then size becomes comparative to a grain of sand. Even that comparison is still inadequate, even if we shrink the earth to a nanoparticle (a billionth of an inch), it wouldn't match up. The bottom line to the argument that we are alone in the universe, like the line from the movie 'Contact', "seems like an awful waste of space!"

Fortunately, to tell this story, we only need to deal with the Milky Way. Given the assumption you would not relate to other galaxies in the vastness of interstellar space anyway. The most significant aspect of this story lies in our own backyard so to speak, meaning our solar system, the earth and our nearest celestial neighbor, the moon.

The earth has quite a colorful history as I have outlined in the preface and introduction. From the most conservative point of view, geologically, it is approximately 4 billion years old. That is based upon carbon decay analysis. This period is only relative to the planet we know of now, not its original form before 4 billion years ago. Anthropologists, archeologists and geologists are a strange lot and suffer from very narrow viewpoints about history and observable facts in front of their face.

In a few examples presented here, ancient civilizations which have proven to be more advanced that our modern civilization, does not sit well with these scientists. They tend to be curiously stubborn to accept what to most of us would seem obvious.

As they pour over ancient records and written documents from scholars and philosophers who talk of other times and other places, they refer to these accounts as mythological and or legendary tales provided to the 'children' of the time as bedtime stories. Of course, there are a few rogue investigators that have differed from the mainstream point of view, but they are as voices in the wind and mostly discarded as heretics or worse, crackpots.

Troy was believed to be a mythical place until they finally uncovered evidence of its actual place in history. A few decades before, there were movements to try and determine if the stories told in the Bible were just that, stories but the demand of evangelicals had a vested interest to prove the authenticity of those Biblical stories by funding archeological digs in various places to prove the validity of Biblical scripture. In some cases, places have been identified, but there are still other places that have not been found. So, the conflict between the faithful and the scientists rage on.

Astrophysicists are not above this narcissistic behavior. No one believed that craters were created by astronomical strikes from other celestial objects until a comet sailing toward Jupiter broke into nine pieces like a string of loose pearls on the first encounter with Jupiter. On the comet's second pass proceeded to impact Jupiter like a machine gun firing meteors one after the other. So that erroneous belief was shattered by the Schoemaker-Levy comet incident in July of 1994.

As a student in high school, I would gaze at the Mercator map of the world and wonder about the idea that South America seemed to fit very well with the coastline of Africa. Upon mentioning this in 1958, I was severely scoffed at for even mentioning this preposterous idea. Then a few years later the concept of tectonic plate movement became the subject of great interest, and the geologists began to accept the idea at one time all the continents were joined together, and that mega-continent was called Pangea. I was a teenager. I did not get the chance to say to my scoffing friends later, "Ah ha! you, see? I was right!"

I remember Carl Sagan said, while hosting the program 'Cosmos' in 1980, that there cannot be any life in our solar system because there is no water present anywhere in our vicinity of the galaxy. Yet, the Martian rover running around on the surface of Mars taking pictures recently discovered a virtual ocean under the Martian surface!

Now everyone is excited that Mars may have been inhabited at some time in the past. Poor Percival Lowell, an amateur astronomer who in 1930, after spending millions of his own money building the largest terrestrial telescope in Arizona, looked at Mars and saw canals. Of course, the mainstream astronomers thought he had lost his mind! Now they are willing to admit there were canals on Mars with running water in the distant past.

So, okay what am I saying with all this diatribe? I am preparing you, the reader, for another opportunity to have your view broadened. This will be the darndest story you have ever heard.

In the distant past, the earth had been visited by several extraterrestrials and they narrow down to two species, one is Lyran from Vega, a feline hominid race. The others represent two strains of reptilians, one is from Orion and the other from another planet from our own twin star system. Our sun's twin is a dwarf star, (our system is a binary star system like most solar systems) sitting in the outer most regions of an area called the Kuyper belt. A planet called by the ancient Sumerian civilization 'Nibiru' (which means earth crosser).

An American astronomer by the name of R.S. Harrington plotted the orbital path of the mysterious planet X in 1988. Then, Zacharia Sitkin referred to this 12th planet in his book by the same name, "*The 12th Planet*" translated from Sumerian clay tablets defining its existence, in an ancient historical account 6,000 years ago, determined its approximate orbital path through our solar system. According to the translations by Sitchen, the reptilian visitors related to the Sumerians all about their home world when they came here 450,000 years ago.

The reptilians were called the Anunnaki by the Sumerians (those from the sky came to earth).

There have been many signs of extraterrestrial visitations depicted by early hominids on earth in their cave pictographs by many early civilizations around the globe. There have been 120, 000,000 sightings of UFOs and UWOs (underwater UFOs) of which some 20,000 have been seen landing since the first saucer crash in New Mexico in 1947. The first report was an honest report by the local newspaper. It didn't take long for the US Army Airforce to debunk the report and called it a weather balloon.

When some 50 saucers flew over the capitol in Washington in 1952, President Truman became alarmed by the potential military threat and formulated a special top-secret group called the Majestic 12. Their efforts for capture and retrieval of fallen spacecraft have been the subject of a serious coverup by the government ever since this time. Intelligence organizations such as the CIA and the National Defense and National Security Agencies have created a disinformation program,to help keep these incidents under wraps also to keep the development of secret aircraft created at area 51 in Nevada, from becoming public knowledge, a national security risk. Much of these programs are now under DARPA, (Defense Advanced Research Projects Agency) an arm of the military industrial complex that funds black projects without any congressional oversight.

Among Ufologists there has been an increasing interest in those incidents of UFO appearances which involve abductions. Beginning with the first case such as Betty and Barney Hill who upon returning home from visiting friends and relatives after a few days, thought it strange that their return trip took several hours longer than it should have. They felt physically ill and strange some days later. So, they sought help from a hypnotherapist who regressed them back to the night of the missing time. To their utter surprise and horror, they both recounted being stopped by a UFO on the road and taken aboard the alien ship during that time.

At the time most people found their story as not very credible. However, according to Betty's story, she recounted having had conversations with the captain of the alien ship. She asked him where they came from. He showed her a star map and revealed their home star and planetary system even defined certain trade routes illustrated on the map. During the recounting of her experience while under hypnosis, she redrew what she saw aboard the ship and astrophysicists superimposed her drawing later upon several star maps and one matched almost perfectly to the Zeta Reticula system, some 40 light years away. After that confirmation, their story enjoyed a bit more consideration though in the main, most remained skeptical about their story.

In another case, a group of lumberjacks working in the woods of northern Arizona witnessed a UFO hovering over the pines while leaving the work site. Everyone was scared to death and couldn't wait to leave the area but one man by the name of Travis Walton became overwhelmed by curiosity. He left the pickup truck to get a closer look much to the chagrin of his fellow workers. As Travis approached the saucer and stood under neath the vehicle, a bright light shown down on him, and he was dragged into the saucer and the saucer left.

Authorities accused the lumberjack party of killing Travis and disposing of the body. They protested enough for their lawyer to demand a lie detector test.

Much to the amazement of the local authorities, they all passed their detector tests. The charges were dropped. Travis remained missing for 5 days until one night, he was found huddling near a gas station without any clothing and in shock.

Travis recounted his horrible experience aboard while the aliens attempted to perform several experiments on his body. Despite their restraining him, he resisted breaking free and accosted some of the aliens and injured them. They decided he was not worth the trouble and returned him to earth.

Over the years there have been many reports of abductions of people, but some have been taken to secret underground alien laboratories on earth, where they were dismembered and or genetically joined with other animal lifeforms from earth and were never heard of again. One such secret military base situated in Dulce, New Mexico is purported to be a secret base of Army and Alien operations located deep into the Archuleta Mesa.

A Civil engineer by the name of Phil Schneider was contracted by the US government to build a deep underground facility near Dulce. He was busy drilling holes for the pilon supports when he kept ruining his drilling equipment. He descended in a portable elevator to examine the source of the problem with a military guard and discovered that there was already a reinforced concrete facility located under the ground where he was drilling. When he descended to the bottom, he encountered several aliens, he drew a weapon and fired upon one of them and killed him. The other aliens returned fire with their own weapons burning away part of his hand and wounding him in the side.

After his recovery, he joined together with other Ufologists on tour to tell his story. By his own recognition, his whistle blowing efforts against the secret alien-military joint operations would probably shorten his life came true. 3 months later he was found dead in his hotel room tied with his hands behind a chair and strangled with a rubber hose. The authorities defined his death as suicidal!

Statistically, more than 100,000 people have disappeared without a trace every year, and some of those have been children. Nome, Alaska is a region known as a UFO hot spot. Nome, Alaska is so isolated from civilization because there are no roads that can reach the town other than by air. Many reports have come from Nome about missing people in recent years. There are countless places of UFO profound activity, such as Mount Shasta in California. In addition, there have been many sightings of UWO (Underwater objects entering and leaving certain areas of water near California and other places.

Despite obvious attempts to placate the public

with promised disclosure, there will never be a willingness to fully disclose the alien agenda here. The governments are involved in their presence and their agreements to allow abductions in exchange for technological advantage is a matter of record.

   A reporter questioned Werner Von Braun once about Germany's extremely advanced technology over the US during the war. Von Braun simply pointed to the sky and said, "we had help."

For millions of years the Lyran Lunar station crew silently managed to keep the lunar station in its proper tidal lock position and orbit without incident. Alien activity on the moon was kept to the rear (dark) side always. In addition to the lunar station, the Lyran satellite orbited over the polar region (called the black knight) providing technical data about earth's stability geologically, as well as observing the natural evolution unfolding on the planet. The satellite was fully automated and required no maintenance from the lunar crew while it monitored and analyzed the state of the planet and its development.

For a time, life on earth remained primitive. From the beginning of the Pleistocene period, the Lyrans intended to accelerate evolution again. The reptilian lifeforms were first to arise dominating the evolutionary path. The Lyrans wanted to steer evolution on this planet in a different direction, giving way to more sophisticated mammalian development.

They introduced an extinction event by dragging a large asteroid (6 miles in diameter) to impact the earth. This reset and redirected the evolutionary pathway by fire engulfing the land mass Pangea. Then they reseeded the oceans again with more sophisticated lifeforms, setting the Cambrian explosion into action.

After this period of earth's early history, the situation became more complicated. The emergence of early primates eventually developed into bipedal hominids as expected. Originally, the Lyrans considered colonizing earth themselves, taking direct involvement in the hominid development toward a spiritual direction. The earth was still unstable. So, they decided it wasn't a good time for them. That is when other species took interest and began to arrive to investigate this unusually beautiful planet.

When the Anunnaki came 450,000 years ago, following the breakup of the mega-continent of Pangea, they settled their colonies in the newly formed African region. Then immediately began mining for gold. That was not a problem for the Lyrans. They continued to monitor the surface development confident that all was still according to their plan. Even so, the earth hominids were not advanced enough to realize they were being monitored.

When the Anunnaki interfered with the hominid development by altering their genetic patterns, this increased their potential artificially. Now, the expected evolutionary pattern of the hominids no longer followed their expected evolutionary timetable. The Lyrans suddenly found themselves in uncharted waters. While the Lyrans considered this unexpected development, the Anunnaki took a stronger interest in the progression of the hominids. They needed a strong work force of slaves to do their mining. The Lyrans noticed that the internal affairs of the Anunnaki became intertwined with their slave laborers.

The Anunnaki realized they would need to feed their slaves and would need to teach them agriculture. Then for the slaves to be effective in the mining process, they would need to teach them their language as well as the skills to operate Anunnaki equipment. The hominids (called Adamites, from the Anunnaki term Adamu or first Adam) were now Homo-Sapiens, rapidly growing in intellect with greater skills to become a force to reckon with. In addition, the Homo Sapiens could not reproduce until the Anunnaki continued to alter the DNA of the 'Adamite' hominids so, they could reproduce in greater numbers by necessity. However, their reproductive behavior far outstripped Anunnaki expectations.

Then more disturbing events unfolded when 5th density beings became enthralled by the beauty of the female Adamites. These 5th density beings came to earth and copulated with the Homo-Sapien hybrids to create giant offspring (the Biblical term for these offspring were Nephilim).

The situation was rapidly getting out of hand. The Lyrans felt this unnatural imbalance brought on the need to intercede. The Lyran lunar crew were about to contact the home world about this dilemma of evolutionary interference when King Anu took matters into his own hands.

Fear of the growth of the Adamite herds rebelling and the appearance of giant children from 5th density engagement with the Adamites, King Anu of the Anunnaki became alarmed by this situation. The King decided to eliminate the adamites and the giants that roamed the planet all at once. He ordered an extinction event of his own. This was accomplished with a massive flood by altering the earth's axis suddenly causing a global tidal wave.

The Anunnaki remained suspended above the earth in their ships waiting until the waters receded. They returned and began the restoration of Iridu, their original colony location. They erected pyramids as new landing beacons for their cargo ships. They successfully irradicated almost all life on the earth which eliminated the Lyran need to intercede. They returned to the mines with their own Igiggi workers to remove much of the gold already excavated and brought it back to the mothership parked in low orbit around Mars, their way station.

Lord Enki, first son of King Anu, sympathetic to the Adamites had secretly provided an escape plan for Gilgemesh (referred to in the Jewish historical narrative as Noah) which included his family along with several DNA vials of animal life needed to help replenish the ecological balance on the planet. Their lifeboat (the Arc) finally landed on the top of Mount Ararat one hundred days later, in what would later become Turkey. The Adamites would flourish again, beyond Anunnaki awareness. After a few thousands of years passed, King Anu ordered most of the fleet back to their home planet Nibiru. Anu left several generals behind to oversee their colonies and to handle the remainder of the mined gold.

All presence of the Anunnaki were gone except for one, general Yahweh. He decided to remain and continued to rule over the area now known as Palestine. He became known by the Tribe of Judah Adamites as their one true 'Storm God.' His Aruku ship was perched on top of Mount Sainai (seen by Moses as the burning bush) remaining only to free his dedicated followers from the regent of Egypt, known as Pharoah, before he left the planet.

Meanwhile

Life aboard the Lunar station returned to normal. As the Homo-Sapien hybrids continued to flourish expanding their occupation in various parts of the emerging land masses. The crew set about to recalibrate their polar satellite to continue the monitoring of the earth's new life cycle.

Later

While the Lunar crew were busy observing the last Dryas (ice age) cycle now in its final stages of reseeding, they were unaware that the earth was under great scrutiny by the Chi Ahkar empire. The reptilian armada sat at the outer LeGrange point waiting for the signal to advance their invasion forces to take the earth for all its resources and begin the enslavement of humanity.

Elbek stood determined at the helm of the command platform of the mammoth Chi Ahkar star destroyer with his mate, Erdane standing proudly beside him, being the first female to accompany a raiding party. Her presence was not well accepted by his crew and against accepted battle protocol. There was descent quietly brewing among the crew and the second in command, Riga, jealous of Elbek's command position, quietly organized some of his loyalists with talk of rebellion leading to mutiny. This was not unusual with the reptilian military ascension to power among lower ranks. Riga stiffened with his courage to confront Elbek in front of the crew.

"Commander Elbek, Rigo commanded sternly with a low but demanding voice.

You are in violation of command order Zeta 103, of the Military code, no females are allowed aboard a command vessel during combat operations!"

Elbek attempted to dismiss his second with aloofness, chuckling a little, and declared flatly.

"As usual Riga, your timing is always with poor judgement. And this is not the time."

Riga leaned forward aggressively. He grunted with a disapproving scowl.

Then Elbek turned slightly and said,

"Really! Are you sure you want to do this now?"

Elbek slowly wrapped his hand around the pistol grip of his laser pistol snugly tucked under his belt. Then he turned again to peer out through the large viewing port at the target planet before them.

He purposefully did not acknowledge his second's challenge and continued to peer through the large viewing port while addressing the navigator.

"Navigator, have you the correct coordinates of our advanced landing position?"

The navigator said nervously,

"Yes commander, it is secured."

Two of Riga's allies, Yeke and Zorig stepped forward to guard Riga's flanks.

Before Riga could draw his pistol, Elbek turned quickly to strike Zorig in the neck with his first shot, causing Zorig's blue blood to splash wildly free in the air, while his large torso fell behind Riga with a loud metallic thud to the command deck floor. Then one of the crew, Delger, loyal to Commander Elbek, raised his laser rifle and shot Yeke in the shoulder forcing Yeke to lose his weapon while dropping to one knee.

Riga stood alone, quietly facing the muzzle of Elbek's pistol now aimed at his head. Riga lowered his drawn weapon and lowered his head in submission.

Elbek turned to Delger and commanded.

"Take this poor excuse of a soldier to a holding cell below. I will deal with him later!"

Delger nodded.

"Yes Commander."

Elbek pointed forward with a strong thrust of his claw.

"Engage Navigator!"

The Navigator responded.

"Engaging thrusters, commander."

The thrusters began to whine and then explode into a thunderous roar pushing the massive hulk of the star destroyer forward as it began the descent to

## The Chi Ahkar Gambit

the planet's surface.

### Meanwhile

The lunar station crew burst into a flurry of chaos scurrying about trying to cope with the invading force, having no way of stopping the charge except only to helplessly observe the military action occurring before them. The communications center sent the signal of alarm to their home planet in the Vega system. They nervously awaited a response, but there was only silence from Lyra. The silence signaled the obvious shock from this horrible event unfolding. It was a seeming eternity when their reply returned.

"Continue to observe and do not try to engage in any way. We do not want to lose our satellite, nor do we want the Chi Ahkar to render the lunar station disabled in any way. We are not prepared to engage with the Chi Ahkar at this time. So, Stand down Lunar Station."

The Lyran crew aboard the lunar station quietly watched as several Chi Ahkarwar destroyers passed by the lunar station and descended upon a peaceful planet yet unaware of the doom about to arrive. The hominids were wholly inequipped to deal with the Chi Ahkar invasion force and would soon be in their captivity.

                  Meanwhile

On the surface, the hominids starred at the oncoming number of ominous objects filling their skies with the blackness and thunderous sounds of impending doom, not realizing the true nature of what was about to become the nature of their future.

The colonies of Adamites began to scurry in all directions now frightened about not knowing where to run or where to hide from the invading monsters. Their intuition screaming inside their heads and hearts with helplessness. They knew they were trapped without any possibility of escape.

As the huge ships touched down, the main bay doors opened wide like jaws containing these lethal predators waiting to swallow up their pray. Then out of the ships thousands of the reptilian horde poured out like rivers, a nightmare of repulsive monsters armed with fire sticks (laser rifles) firing over the heads of these poor indigenous creatures being rounded up like cattle into hastily built electronic force fields.

There was little or no resistance from the indigenous people now paralyzed with fear of their captors, wondering when they will be slain and beaten or worse, eaten for dinner. Then they watched as the young ones were trapped separate from their elders. So, their worst fears were realized, it would be their children that would suffer the worst fate, for these monsters drooled when gazing upon them. It was confirmed with horror, that the young that would become their food.

The first Star Destroyer sat down in the great Abzu (Africa) Plain very near the mouth of the Euphrates River. The exit doors to the rear of the craft opened wide exuding a strange air of confidence, of absolute power and authority without question and without any fear or caution about encountering anything or anyone in the way of meaningful resistance, an image that could be compared to an apex predator yawning before a meal.

The metal creaked making a grinding noise as the bay doors revealed the darkened interior. A disturbing sound blurted from inside signaling the time for the foot soldiers to disembark from the ship. They began to pour out of the ship in rows of two by the thousands. They all wore black armor and dark blue tunics underneath, giving an extra accent to their dark green and bluish scales.

They stood in two lines facing each other providing a long and secure pathway from the ship. The landing pilons kept the hull of the ship high from the surface. So, the exit required a long ramp extending from the rear deck. The first battalion took their position as front guard while the second battalion proceeded to follow in the same pattern. The ship's Commander appeared after several minutes, stopping only to gaze at the might of the troops sprawled before him. The leader stood strong, seeming to loom larger compared to the others below him. He stepped forward onto the ramp embracing this new world like a hero-hunter that has captured his prey, branding a proud and stout posture of dominance and almost regal quality.

The Chi Ahkar species are militaristic. Though it is a mighty empire engulfing thousands of planets in several hundred-star systems, the hierarchy was strict and followed a system of rigid rules of behavior among the ranks, even their language was honorific to define the sharp differences within ranks and their privileges.

There was no recognized royalty per se, but their system of organization began with the generals, commanding the ships and their troop battalions. There were planetary leaders forming the basis of a large group of executives with supreme authority within a combined council of worlds. Important decisions were delt with in a council format but final words for action fell to the regional leaders and handed down to the commanders of the Destroyer fleet.

Each Star Destroyer arrived about one day apart. The initial landings were not far from each other at first. Many scout ships were immediately deployed to survey the surrounding areas to determine the lifeforms present and to assess their relative numbers. Then troop assignments were given and instructions for rounding up and separating various species by obvious intelligence and required function.

Reptilian engineers brought out many devices from the ship for the analysis of soil, and atmosphere. The terrain of the earth was still heavily masked because of the previous depositing of sediment from the flood waters that poured over the lands in the last Dryas event. The large ice mantels still covered much of the existing surface of the continents which supported colder temperatures. This consideration was important for long term plans for mining operations because these reptilian species were not warm-blooded humanoids.

These creatures lived in solar systems spanning

great distances from their main sequence stars. Earth was sitting uncomfortably close to Sol in this system. The coldness of the Ice mantels contrasted with the intolerable brightness of the sequence star during daylight hours. The daylight brightness demanded that they wear their helmet visors to shield their sensitive eyes from the sun. Mining schedules adapted to night conditions which required the need for artificial illumination of the work areas, thus giving the appearance of small cities around the camps. Night operations also created stress with the problem of keeping warm on the surface, a condition only slightly alleviated for underground mining as the condition in the tunnels remained steady with small temperature variations. This placed an additional burden on the ship's power supply requirements. So, setting up additional external fusion power stations became a priority for the mining camps.

There was so much earth debris from the flood, the original Anunnaki facilities could not be utilized at first, not until the debris was removed. Large earth movers and excavating equipment became essential.

A total of five destroyers landed originally. This was standard deployment for first time arrival to targets designated for invasion forces. Once the areas marked for settlement had been established, two of the destroyers remained on the surface while the other three destroyers, having offloaded the rest of the heavy equipment, dusted off to low earth orbits.

The first the command and control center for all operations functioned from the master helm of the ship. All communications to the other ships and the ground crew emanated from there. The master helm room situated as the most forward compartment nearest the bow of the ship, was quite large comprising two partial decks with a large opening descending to the lower deck of the ship. Banks of computer stations and monitoring of the ship's interior, power regulation, engine control and navigation as well as the exterior views were displayed by many large viewing screens wrapped around each control deck snuggly tucked into their own individual compartments separated by narrow bulkheads.

Engineers and operations personnel moved about

the helm area focused on their tasks at hand. In the center of the upper command deck was a large circular table comprising a holographic projection of the areas surrounding the ship as well as the nearby ongoing excavating operations. A few engineers stood around discussing the progress of their recovery work while adjusting specific views of the operations from control panels mounted on the rim of the table.

Commander Elbek stood near the front viewports of the ship with his claws clenched behind his withers while he starred pensively at the terrain outside. It was night and he thought to himself, 'this planet reminded him of one of the moons of the star Aldebaran.' A feeling of regret moved past his two hearts pumping blue blood throughout his body. He was long overdue for a well-deserved relief, but his last successful campaign on Rigel made a strong impression with the council that demanded his presence on this mission to Terra, their name for earth, a necessity.

He knew that any resistance to an assignment offered by the council was a great honor and should be accepted with the utmost gracious attitude, if not outright enthusiasm. Anything less from this kind of reaction would have cast doubt about his devotion to the empire. Officers of his rank were expected to always present the highest degree of perfect behavior. The very basis of life within the Chi Ahkar society was the corner stone of their continued success as a formidable force in the galaxy.

Though language was used, telepathic communication was preferred. Any kind of private thought would need to be guarded, especially if those thoughts could be construed by others nearby as traitorous or unsupportive to the cause. Command positions were revered and jealously admired. These positions of authority were also subject to the possibility of a challenge by a would-be aspiring combatant. One had to be constantly vigilant and at the same time demonstrating a sense of extreme and fierce confidence.

Friends were few in military life, relegated to those of similar rank. Like all military societies, officers spent most of their time with other officers and little or no time fraternizing with those of lower rank, and especially never with foot soldiers. In fact, their attitude toward foot soldiers was a necessary and unrewarding duty. They were often looked upon as odorous slime, merely useful maggots to do their bidding.

The ships scanners revealed a considerable number of ore, in particular, gold. Large quantities of this ore were indicated near the surface and showing a refined quality as well. This was truly surprising and unusual in the Chi Ahkar experience. When word got back to the council about this, it only reinforced the council's decision to make this solar system of Terra their next choice for acquisition to the empire. Gold was an element highly regarded in the galaxy and prized for its value to use as chattel for the exchange of goods and services as well as a good bargaining chip to entice other races to join the empire in its advance toward an ever growing and powerful presence in the galaxy.

The indigenous population of homo sapiens preferred to remain at a healthy distance from these new intruders, well hidden within the dense foliage of the foothills. To the Terran Hominids, these creatures were so unlike their previous captors of old. All memories of their ancestral captors remained dimly in the minds of older generations and now remained as myths and legends. Though they were also reptilian according to their rudimentary records of their ancestors, these creatures were an exaggeration to horrific proportions.

   By comparison, their ancestors related to their benefactors, the Anunnaki, as somewhat benign teachers, even though they were slaves then. They were protected and cared for by their masters. The cuneiform writing and pictographs on the walls of these cave dwellers, described them as large as the newcomers. The newcomers possessed a fearsome appearance and did not inspire a strong sense of anything but terror. There was much discussion amongst the elders of the Adamite refugees of the great younger Dryas.

   Clothed in furs and accustomed to the harsh environment left behind as their legacy from the Anunnaki decree for their ultimate extinction. They were thankful of their meager existence and glad to be alive. Their existence halted from the agrarian farming. The Adamites returned to the necessity of

## Mining the Old Camp

becoming hunter-gatherers again. Now they were smarter and enjoyed their inherited cleverness brought about by their benefactors. They knew how to fabricate better tools and better weapons against their predators. However, they realized that their crude weapons were no match against these formidable warriors which wielded sharp swords and burning light weapons.

The scout ships had no difficulty located and identifying the adamites hidden within the foothills by virtue of their heat scanners. It didn't take long for them to round them up in greater numbers. The Chi Ahkar did not speak the adamite language, but they had the advantage of universal translators which were quickly adapted to the adamite language. Once the soldiers realized that the mental capacity to withstand the force of reptilian mind control was minimal, managing the captives was relatively easy by telepathy.

Some of the excavating equipment left behind by the Anunnaki still lay buried within the thick silt. The adamites joined together to dig out the equipment thinking that this might serve to alter their relationship to their captors, but the Chi

In fact, the suggestion that claiming ownership of this new world in absentia of the ruling class of the empire made logical sense and should the armada return, the mining colony would be able to negotiate on their own terms which included amnesty for their independence and defiance to the empire.

Golthon was in a tough position and needed to weigh the potential of the troop demands and seriously considered if the empire would accept. Their declaration of an independent mining colony perhaps serving the empire in their own independent way might be feasible, but these were questions without answers leaving those in command positions at risk should they return less than eager to accept their proposal.

No decision was made in the short term. After two millennia had past, without any response to their messages sent through hyperspace transmissions, Golthon finally relented to his troop's demands and declared Terra, as a separate sovereign. Heretofore technically an independent colony of the Empire until word was received otherwise. In the men time, the conclusion was that the rebellion in the home world turned to the possible fall or decline in the empire of a thousand worlds. The mere idea was inconceivable that their empire could have fallen. They were unaware that the rebel forces were supported by the alliance of the Lyran delegation forcing the Chi Ahkar back into the Orion base of operations.

The reptilian colony grew in number and continued to tunnel vast networks of domiciles extending from the great Abzu to other continents. Those domiciles still exist today, and they uncovered many huge underground chambers affording them the opportunity to create hubs of cities and the consolidation of their species into a thriving civilization. Their aim is still to develop hybrid offspring that can sustain the harsh environment of the surface. So, throughout the centuries that passed since their arrival, they continue to abduct human life on the surface to carry on their genetic experiments. Certain agreements have been forged to facilitate these abductions I exchange for technological assistance to the shadow government on the surface.

Before the lead command ship dusted off commander Elbek called a meeting with the colonels of the battalions that were to be left behind to mind the continuation of the mining operations until their return.

The two Colonels came aboard and ascended to the command deck immediately, finding General Elbek standing before the main viewing port with claws clenched behind his withers.

General Elbek then turned to face his surface command crew. Ereok and Golthan stood silently at attention, awaiting their master's orders.

Elbek began ceremoniously.

"You have been chosen with a great honor and duty to guard the empire's bounty here. You are expected to continue the mining operations while at the same time increasing output in a measured fashion admirable to the fleet, keeping in mind that your continued presence on this strange world will in no way embarrass this fleet or the empire.

"Urgent matters have arisen in the Mica system which the supreme council has declared of greater importance requiring our assistance. A small but significant upstart rebellion has attempted to overthrow the battalions in charge of one of the moons of Altairon, a strategic outpost that has some of our most valued weapons and surveillance equipment, which if captured, could weaken our alliance with the indigenous species in the nearby worlds."

Ereok stiffened in his posture and slapped his breastplate vigorously, stating.

"By your command, we shall not disappoint you commander."

Then Golthan followed in like manner saying.

"I too will ensure the troops abide by your wishes Commander. Golthan continued.

"Sir, we will make sure our work ethic continues in the same light of your inspired leadership and continued success of this mining operation to be the beacon of the empire's outreach."

Elbek turned away from both officers and continued his view through the helm's viewport to monitor the progress to expedite their plans to return to the Mica system.

"You may return to your duties now. You are dismissed."

The commanders slapped their breast plates

ceremoniously together and left the helm promptly.

Elbek's adjutant Heog turned to the Colonel and commented.

"Sir, do you think the rebellion will be easy to restore order in the realm quickly?

Elbek paused and returned sarcastically,

"Do you have somewhere else to go Lieutenant?"

Heog bowed his head for a moment and responded meekly.

" No sir, I only meant to express my concern for the realm and the surprising need for our immediate return seemed to speak something of a more serious situation, which Command is not telling us, Sir."

Elbek noted his adjutant's concern and replied enforcing his confidence in the decisions of Command.

"Our formidable forces are unmatched in the galaxy and I'm quite sure Command has everything well in hand, perhaps they want a show of force to the rebel contingent."

Heog smiled and replied.

"Yes of course Sir, you are right as always."

Then Elbek inquired changing the subject.

"Lieutenant, have you stowed my gear on the lead ship yet?

Heog responded smartly, "absolutely Sir"

Golthan and Ereok stood at the edge of the landing field to watch the lead, and two other ships dust off to space.

Golthan turned to Ereok and spoke.

"Come my friend we have much to do now that the brass has vacated."

Ereok laughed.

Golthan laid out further excavation plans but included mining underground facilities for an extended stay on this strange planet of the bright star. Surface dwelling would not be possible for them except for mining at night. It would be necessary for them to create underground operations and as well as living quarters for the troops, then they could transport the gold to a storage facility on the surface with minimum exposure.

These plans for further development of the mining camp were considered only temporary as their expectation for their armada to return to this outpost was quite high. It was only after several hundred years had passed that questions regarding their position and the fate of the mining colony now began to expand to longer term conditions.

Time extended from decades of no contact to millennia without word from the home world. Many of the troops began to complain to Golthon. The condition of their plight on this strange world now appeared more like a rescue mission. Many believed the decision to abandon this mining project seemed quite plausible. A demand that the leadership of the mining crew be altered and compensation was in order, following the demand that a separate colony, standing alone from the empire be established. Further, that a new disposition be declared with regards to the ownership of the mines and the gold extracted by their efforts should now belong to the miners in compensation for their continued efforts. The troops dared to suggest a complete separation from the empire which would certainly be viewed by the empire as rebellion and treason subject to trial and termination to all those
involved in the insurrection. The warriors turned miners ceased to see themselves as a part of the

Chi Ahkar Empire. In fact, the suggestion that claiming ownership of this new world in absentia of the ruling class of the empire made logical sense and should the armada return, the mining colony would be able to negotiate on their own terms which included amnesty for their independence and defiance to the empire.

Golthon was in a tough position and needed to weigh the potential of the troop demands and seriously considered if the empire would accept. Their declaration of an independent mining colony perhaps serving the empire in their own independent way might be feasible, but these were questions without answers leaving those in command positions at risk should they return less than eager to accept their proposal.

No decision was made in the short term. After two millennia had past, without any response to their messages sent through hyperspace transmissions, Golthon finally relented to his troop's demands and declared Terra, as a separate sovereign. Heretofore technically an independent colony of the Empire until word was received otherwise. In the men time, the conclusion was that the rebellion in the home world turned to the possible fall or decline in the empire of a thousand worlds. The mere idea was inconceivable that their empire could have fallen. They were unaware that the rebel forces were supported by the alliance of the Lyran delegation forcing the Chi Ahkar back into the Orion base of operations.

The reptilian colony grew in number and continued to tunnel vast networks of domiciles extending from the great Abzu to other continents. Those domiciles still exist today, and they uncovered many huge underground chambers affording them the opportunity to create hubs of cities and the consolidation of their species into a thriving civilization. Their aim is still to develop hybrid offspring that can sustain the harsh environment of the surface. So, throughout the centuries that passed since their arrival, they continue to abduct human life on the surface to carry on their genetic experiments. Certain agreements have been forged to facilitate these abductions I exchange for technological assistance to the shadow government on the surface.

## Who Goes There

The presence of reptilians from another world living on or in the earth remains today as a tapestry of myth and legend. There is ample archeological evidence in the form of art and sculptures from older civilizations long since buried in the dust of time. Only a few brave scientists have the courage to speak out regarding what they know about the evidence of their continued existence here. Unfortunately, their credibility is often challenged as a fringe of conspiratorial opinion and sided with other urban legends of a neanderthal-like creature known as 'big foot'. In the main, no anthropologist or archeologist will say anything that would destroy or hamper their reputation.

Urban legends of sitings by campers and explorers of the various wilderness areas in the United States federal parklands report encounters with monsters that look like human reptiles complete with webbed feet, claws for hands with scale-like skin. They are hunters and carnivores, exude a strong odor and very territorial, intelligent and cunning and quite aggressive and threatening to those who have accidentally discovered their lairs in the wild. Many who have camped in the wilderness have heard their cries and growls at night.

There is a strong government agenda to hide their clandestine agreements with these creatures. Their joint underground secret laboratories where both reptilian and human scientists work side by side in a cooperative effort, continue according to whistle blowers who have been involved with these secret labs and have lived long enough to tell their tales of truth.

The conspiracies regarding these reptilian creatures offer further descriptions of their enate abilities, which may include temporary shape shifting and presenting themselves as actual human members of the shadow government manipulating world affairs in secret. Conspiracy promoters suggest that they shape shift to exist among humans, however, because of their limitations on the surface severely limit their time on the surface. It is more than likely they have cloned humanoid bodies to accomplish this intermingling.

Meanwhile, their presence is cloaked by subordinate groups such as, the Council of 13, the Committee of 300, the Illuminati, and the

Bilderberg Group which meet secretly in Europe every year hosting heads of state from many nationalities coming together to discuss the future of mankind and the earth under their rulership and control.

Since this prison condition has lasted on earth for many millennia, The Galactic Federation of Worlds has now adopted a new policy regarding interference. Non-interference has been replaced by the choice to remove the reptilian presence from earth and this solar system permanently within the next decade. This of course will be proceeded by a full disclosure of this extraterrestrial presence and their agreements heretofore debunked by the shadow government and the military industrial complex.

Further evidence as to their agenda comes from the statistical records of missing persons, who vanish without a trace every year and this number is more than a million humans involving men, women and children. It is noted that the reptilians have great mental powers and collectively can wield tremendous control over the thoughts and actions of the masses of humans on the surface.

They use their technology to accomplish this also. Unfortunately, the reptilians being carnivores, enjoy the tasty morsels of flesh and blood of young human children to feed on.

The reptilians also feed off strong negative emotions of greed, fear, violence and hatred. They manipulate nations and promote wars all over the world just for this purpose. These emotional energies are like a drug for them. They are addicted.

There are many reptilian species that represent hybrids throughout the galaxy, and many are peaceful in nature, but the Chi Ahkar are the oldest species and the most ruthless and brutal of the known 3D universe commonly known as the Dracos and reside in their home world in the Orion star system.

They are tall, on average between 8 and 10 feet in height. They are very muscular with a skin that is tough and covered with bluish green scales. The Draco have eyes that have slitted pupils with an orange retina. Other hybrids have round pupils. Some have wings which allow flight, but all have a tail.

The truth of the reptilian presence represents a

vast system of control over this planet which makes earth a prison planet. They use the equipment they have installed on the dark side of the moon to assist in maintaining this control and their dominance also extends even beyond the human physical existence.

Their history goes back billions of years. They reside mainly in the Orion constellation with Betelgeuse as their main sequence star.
Though their empire stretches far beyond to the Mica system, with thousands of planets under their control and enslavement. They are strong and powerful. Most species fear them. Many have fought them like the Lyrans and have almost become extinct.

They are fierce warriors and quite cunning. Their technology is advanced far above many other advanced races. Their star destroyers are mammoth sized ships that can be as long as 3 miles long and their weaponry is quite sophisticated.

The fact that the Galactic Federation of Planets think twice about going against them is only bolstered by a united front of some 50 other races, otherwise they try to steer clear of any confrontations unless necessary.

The main reason they have not approached earth and this system before is because that the Military Industrial Complex that comprises the bulk of the leadership on earth stand to keep them here as they continue their alliances with them for mutual benefit.

# Assault on Lunar Station

The Lyran lunar crew were busy recalibrating the north-polar orbiting satellite known on their logs as XRL2-1. Later, humans of the 20th century would name it the 'Black Knight'. This calibration was necessary every sixth passage of the satellite due to the requirements of the lunar station synchronization needed for adjusting to declination perturbations or changes of the third planet called Terra.

The main reason for this was the artificial moon needed to be larger in diameter to make up for the gravitational differentials as compared to the original organic mineral moon that was destroyed. A moon that is solid reacts to the quantum more slowly whereas a hollow sphere is by its construction, lighter and therefore more easily influenced by external forces of the central sun such as solar storms occurring every 11 years. Also, the magnetic flux artificially created needed to be harmonically balanced to compensate for the inherent wobble of Terra's axis that defined the precession of its rotation.

Though the apparatus that kept the artificial moon from a slow descent and decay of its orbital elevation and deviation, needed to be automated, spurious alterations of high energy space-born random field fluctuations pouring out of interstellar exo-celestial events would often generate and stream powerful cosmic rays interrupting the control feedback loop creating an unsteady orbital pattern.

This process also interrupted the smoothness of the tidal lock to maintain the forward-facing side toward Terra, which was always critical, otherwise the slippage would cause a creeping in rotation revealing the back or dark side. That would be obvious to those on the surface of Terra revealing the Lyran presence. That revelation would be troublesome to explain for the surface inhabitants in later stages of their evolutionary cycles of animal life when that life would become sentient.

Crews would be rotated systematically measured by every two sideral rotations of Terra around the main sequence star called Sol. This went along fine for many hundreds-of-thousands of sideral cycles until one day everything stopped cold. The lunar crew became quite chaotic for a time as they were amid troubleshooting the problem when they realized the system was fine.

It would soon become apparent to the crew tha

the problem was not with the Lunar station control center nor was it the fault of any of the crew. Much to their chagrin, the problem was due to the bombardment of a particle beam weapon aimed at the artificial station. The result was an effective way to suspend the normal lunar positioning because of the paralyzing effect of the beam weapon thrust upon the vulnerable satellite by a large Chi Ahkar battle cruiser parked alongside the lunar station.

It was only moments after this that the station was boarded by an elite Chi Ahkar commando team on a mission to take over the station. The crew of the station were shocked at the rapidity by which the team of commandos rushed through out the various inner layers of the station until the entire station was secured under the Chi Ahkar command.

Next the leaders of the invasion force secured the critical crew members having advanced knowledge of the stations inner workings and control systems. The Chi Ahkar did not need to torture the crew members because they possessed advanced mind control techniques to press the crew for all the critical information, they needed to override the systems and bring the station under they're control.

The commando leader signaled the chi Ahkar destroyer commander. He was immediately informed of the success of the take over then he signaled the commanders of the fleet already parked just beyond the Mars orbit.

The Chi Ahkar engineers began to reconfigure the antennas designed to monitor surface life and integrated their own technology into the transmitters and receivers to begin the mind control frequencies geared toward the Terran humanoids on the surface. Thus, the ground plan was well underway for the arrival of the fleet to commence surface deployment of troops to descend to the surface. The next step was to establish their advanced command stations beneath the coastal waters near to every continental plate. Seven suboceanic stations were dropped from the destroyers and the crews were beamed aboard once the fusion power converters were fired up and powering the stations.

It would be a matter of hours when the communication networks tying all substations together were established. Phase one of the invasion was complete.

Once the Lyran planetary analysis scanners were brought on line, they revealed an unanticipated issue through their graviton wave space-time interpreters that this planet was going to be subjected to certain future anomalies that disrupt their plans. A meeting of the commanders of the fleet came together to determine what might be needed to avert these anomalies before they were to unfold.

On the dark side of the moon are several very tall towers extending miles above the lunar surface. NASA a has tried very hard to scrub or blank out by digital retouch and or replacing these objects utilizing digital altering techniques sent back from the moon by lunar landers. Some of these pictures are quite stunning but they appear on sides for a short time before they are removed from public view.

The Chinese lunar lander comes long and captures more evidence of strange towers, rectangular shaped buildings that form localized complexes representing clusters of cities with objects that appear as telescope radio transmitting antennas nearby. The pictures of these objects are never explained and often debunked as faulty camera artifacts identically the way that the government tries to explain many UFO sitings in the past as celestial objects like swamp gas or the planet Venus or Jupiter.

For decades other strange appearances of lights on the moon showing deep inside craters on both the front side and the dark side of the moon. Also, lights traveling across the lunar landscape or apparently flying at low altitudes seen and video photographed by amateur astronomers. Then there are pyramidal shapes standing to extreme heights which cast shadows from sunlight shining upon them clearly indicating 'man-made' or perhaps alien in origin, are anything but naturally formed yet Nasa continues to debunk claims by amateur astronomers of their obvious attributes.

These pictures are evidence that alien antenna equipment has been set up to transmit clandestine signals to earth. The signals are not normally related to radio signals or radar signals we on earth would be able to determine. The nature of these signals is unknown by our engineers and or technicians. The technology utilized with these devices is foreign to our known technology and are using sophisticated encoding techniques involving image generation at very low frequencies comparable to brainwave frequencies. The information encoded within these signals are thought based information signals designed to influence the mental attitudes, perceptions and conceptual content intended to influence the brainwave patterns of humans upon the surface of the earth.

Some of these signals can disturb the natural

balance of brain chemistry and emotional stability that encourage human feelings of anxiety and stress and encourage violent behavior and subtle racial rhetoric as well as, feelings of loneliness, isolation and fear.

These are like secret military weaponry developed by DARPA (Defense Advanced Research Projects Agency) a research arm of the military industrial complex, to demoralize soldiers from fighting during wartime. On earth, some of these infernal weapons can control crowds by using microwave signals to heat the atmosphere at a distance location to thwart military action by an adversary. Some of these weapons generate low frequency sound waves that can lock the jawbone and prevent someone from speaking publicly.

As outrageous as this sounds, it's all quite true. If we shift the technology to the levels of alien origin, they become much more insidious and far more effective. The alien technology can achieve so much more.

The Lyran technology established on the artificial moon hundreds-of-thousands of years ago used to monitor the evolutionary development of biological lifeforms on the planet as well as, monitoring the stability of the Terra itself.

These technologies were non-destructive and harmless to any lifeforms on the surface and within the oceans. But the Chi Ahkar reptilians had usurped these technologies and modified them for their own purposes after they captured these technical facilities and eliminated the Lyran engineers once they learned from them the knowledge of their operations. Their intent was to quickly bring this planet under their control and to dominate the lifeforms on the surface for their own negative goals. Slavery was part of their plan as it was for all systems they brought into their empire.

There has been an outcry from the part of the public that is convinced that the Government is covering up the truth about extraterrestrial visitation since the 1947 Roswell incident. Though there are thousands of cases of Bonafide reports of UFO sitings from very credible witnesses including airline pilots, and various law enforcement officers across the country in the United States alone, but Mexico, Argentina, The United Kingdom, Australia and Europe to name a few other countries who have also been investigating these incidents and perhaps by mutual agreement, have kept their investigative work under wraps too.

The term Flying Saucer became popular from an eyewitness account of a pilot by the name of Kenneth Arnold. On June 24, 1947, he saw a line of shiny objects flying near Mount Rainier at speeds he estimated to be 1200 miles per hour. They flew grouped together and appear like a saucer tossed across a pond, in a skipping like action. His story carried in several local newspapers. Later the story appeared in popular magazines which copied his comment 'flying like a saucer'. The term stuck, but the term UFO became the official name for the phenomenon.

I believe there is another reason behind the resistance for full disclosure beyond national security interests. The US Military Industrial Complex has a vested interest with regards to their crash retrieval program and their reverse engineering of ET craft to bolster their military weapons development.

With the fall of The Soviet Socialist Republic and Mikhail Gorbachev's leadership time, Significant quantities of previously classified KGB material on UFO investigations detailing alleged Sitings and encounters became available to the public, with some of the reports and materials also came into the possession of the CIA and other intelligence agencies of the US. The release of these materials was gradual and no information as to exactly when this started since the collapse in 1991.

Dr. Steven Greer and associates have been diligent to press for full disclosure supporting many whistle blowers to come forward and testify before congress. Three such witnesses came forward not only to reveal the crash retrieval program but that the government had performed autopsies on dead ET pilots and even mentioned that some that had survived were brought to military installations where they were studied and interrogated.

In 2005, a former Canadian defense minister, Paul Hellyer, urged the governments of other nations to release what he believed was hidden information about UFOs. Hellyer served as defense minister in the sixties. At age 91, he delivered the keynote speech during the Disclosure Canada Tour appearing at the University of Calgary in Montreal, Toronto and Vancouver. He told the audience of more than 400 attendees "much of the media won't touch it." Mr. Hellyer went on to say, "So you just have to keep working away and hope that someday you get a critical mass, and they will say, in one way or another, 'Mr. President or Mr. Prime Minister we want the truth, and we want it now because it affects our lives.'"

At the end of World War II, the Nazi High Command desperately tried to convince Hitler to fully support the weapons of super science, but he retracted his support in favor of spending what resources they had left on ballistic long range rocket development and the advanced Messerschmidt fighter to become a jet powered craft.
Werner Von Braun and others were working on a

wingless circular field propulsion craft called the Hanabu. A scientist by the name of Victor Schauberger had developed a vortex engine that purportedly powered the craft. Three versions were tested in increasing sizes.

Before the beginning of the war, in 1938, more than 50 U-boats (German submarines) were sent to Antarctica by way of Argentina, carrying scientists, engineers and supplies to build a secret base called New Shwabenland under the proposition that it would be a contingency installation if Germany might lose the war.

It is believed after Rear Admiral Byrd had conducted previous expeditions there, Islandic sailors reported to him that German flags were seen flying in the area. So, Admiral Byrd reported to Washington his concern of a second front planned by the Germans. Washington with the US Navy authorized a fourth expedition, called "Operation Highjump," in the summer of 1946–47. This was a full assault flotilla, with the most massive sea and air operation theretofore attempted in Antarctica. It involved 13 ships, including two seaplane tenders and an aircraft carrier, and a total of 25 airplanes.

The plan was to carry out reconnaissance and if any enemy were encountered, they were to engage.

The expedition was to be a 6-month operation but as soon as they approached, several Hanabu craft came out of the Ice pack and obliterated the flotilla. Many men died, several ships were sunk, all by very fast moving and well-armed flying saucer type aircraft. The 25 propeller driven aircraft were completely out maneuvered. Upon his return and debrief, he told Washington that the Germans possessed very advanced aerial craft capable of flying from pole to pole in twenty minutes or less. His report was written in his personal diary which he kept, and the briefing was kept top secret ad the cover story was this expedition was for scientific research only.

It is my belief that full disclosure would never occur because of the 'shadow government' and the 'secret space program' funded by the Military Industrial Complex would never admit to their alliance with aliens existing on earth to this day.

Nick Pope is an English media commentator and former British civil servant.
His job was with the British Government's Ministry

of Defense, and responsible, among other tasks, for investigating UFO phenomena to determine if they had any defense significance. He has since moved to the US and reported on sitings like the Rendlesham Forest incident where two airmen were sent into the forest to investigate a strange light sighted by perimeter guards near the airbase. It was a close encounter when one of the airmen approached the object hovering nearby and touched the craft before it ascended into the sky.

The general feeling is mixed with witnesses wondering if they are friendly or extending a menacing attitude toward humans. Depending on which sitings you hear about it could be either way.

For example, my former wife was driving along the New Jersey turnpike some 50 years ago and noticed what appeared to be a carnival ride off the side of the road drifting in and out of a cluster of trees. Having an intuitive feeling to investigate. She told her friends to pull over. She left the vehicle and crossed the field toward the trees. When she approached the object, it appeared to be bobbing up and down slowly giving it the appearance of some kind of ride. Then she saw the object swing out from the vertical movement and then she realized it was not a ride.

The object was circular and had many lights around its periphery all blinking at various intervals. As it rotated around, she could see several windows mounted above and could partially see three occupants looking at her. They waved at her, and she instinctively waved back. Then the object began to make a whirring sound as it began to change colors, becoming quite bright and immediately shot straight up and out of sight.

When she told me of the story, many years later, I made her write down her description with a crude drawing of the object. She had not reported this to anyone at that time. So, I took the liberty of sending her report to MUFON, (The Mutual UFO Network, a private agency keeping tabs on sightings around the country.

By contrast, another incident occurred during the filming of a rocket launched at a naval base. Two Navy technicians were watching the launch through a powerful telescope and filming it for research records. After the launch, they film was brough back to the lab and developed. It revealed the rocket souring high into the atmosphere when suddenly a UFO appeared and began to fly around it. Then it proceeded fire a laser three times at the nose cone, from three different angles. They brought the film into the viewing room for some officers to see it.

The officers confiscated the film and forced the technicians to sign non-disclosure agreements and warned them not to ever speak of the incident again.

In another case, The Stars and Stipes Military newspaper quoted former Air Force Captain Robert Salas, who was stationed at Maelstrom Air Force base in Montana in 1967. 10 ICBMs he was responsible for suddenly became inoperative while at the same time, security informed him of a mysterious red object in the sky hovering above the silos. Perhaps the alien object was trying to send a strong message that the occupants were not happy about those weapons and the nuclear warheads mounted on top.

The following are excerpts of a warning from President Dwight D. Eisenhower's farewell speech in 1961. Ref. The National Archives:

"Throughout America's adventure in free government, our basic purposes have been to keep the peace; to foster progress in human achievement, and to enhance liberty, dignity and integrity among people and among nations. To strive for less would be unworthy of a free and religious people. Any failure traceable to arrogance, or our lack of comprehension or readiness to sacrifice would inflict upon us grievous hurt both at home and abroad.

Progress toward these noble goals is persistently threatened by the conflict now engulfing the world. It commands our whole attention, absorbs our very beings. We face a hostile ideology-global in scope, atheistic in character, ruthless in purpose, and insidious in method. Unhappily the danger it poses promises to be of indefinite duration. To meet it successfully, there is called for, not so much the emotional and transitory sacrifices of crisis, but rather those which enable us to carry forward steadily, surely, and without complaint the burdens of a prolonged and complex struggle-with liberty at stake. Only thus shall we remain, despite every provocation, on our charted course toward permanent peace and human betterment.

A vital element in keeping the peace is our military establishment. Our arms must be mighty, ready for instant action, so that no potential aggressor may be tempted to risk his own destruction.

Our military organization today bears little relation to that known by any of my predecessors in peace time, or indeed by the fighting men of World War II or Korea.

Until the latest of our world conflicts, the United States had no armaments industry. American makers of plowshares could, with time and as required, make swords as well. But now we can no longer risk emergency improvisation of national defense; we have been compelled to create a permanent armaments industry of vast proportions. Added to this, three and a half million men and women are directly engaged in the defense establishment. We annually spend on military security more than the net income of all United State corporations.

This conjunction of an immense military establishment and a large arms industry is new in the American experience. The total influence economic, political, even spiritual is felt in every city, every state house, every office of the Federal government. We recognize the imperative need for this development. Yet we must not fail to comprehend its grave implications. Our toil, resources and livelihood are all involved; so is the very structure of our society.

In the councils of government, we must guard against the acquisition of unwarranted influence, whether sought or unsought, by the military industrial complex. The potential for the disastrous rise of misplaced power exists and will persist.

We must never let the weight of this combination endanger our liberties or democratic processes. We should take nothing for granted. Only an alert and knowledgeable citizenry can compel the proper meshing of the huge industrial and military machinery of defense with our peaceful methods and goals, so that security and liberty may prosper together.

Akin to, and largely responsible for the sweeping changes in our industrial-military posture, has been the technological revolution during recent decades.

## Disclosure Myth, Dark Agenda

In this revolution, research has become central; it also becomes more formalized, complex, and costly. A steadily increasing share is conducted for, by, or at the direction of, the Federal government.

Today, the solitary inventor, tinkering in his shop, has been overshadowed by task forces of scientists in laboratories and testing fields. In the same fashion, the free university, historically the fountainhead of free ideas and scientific discovery, has experienced a revolution in the conduct of research. Partly because of the huge costs involved, a government contract becomes virtually a substitute for intellectual curiosity. For every old blackboard there are now hundreds of new electronic computers.

The prospect of domination of the nation's scholars by Federal employment, project allocations, and the power of money is ever present and is gravely to be regarded.

Yet, in holding scientific research and discovery in respect, as we should, we must also be alert to the equal and opposite danger that public policy could itself become the captive of a scientific technological elite."

The Military Industrial Complex comprises several major industrial players for example; Lockheed Martin Skunk Works and Martin Marietta, McDonnel Douglas, Sperry-Rand, Monsanto, Fairchild, the National Aeronautics and Space Agency, and DARPA, the Defense Advanced Research Projects Agency, the research and development arm of the complex, as well as the main security agencies such as, the Central Intelligence Agency, the National Security Agency, the Defense Intelligence Agency, the National Reconnaissance Office and Homeland Security are all presently engaged with the development of advanced military hardware and weaponry which are all funded through 'black operations' that have no congressional oversight or management. They control funds of more than 30 trillion dollars annually.
   These operations are cloaked under the national security act and classified top secret with cosmic level provisions for which not even the Whitehouse has clearance. So how did this happen? It began with the crash of a UFO in Roswell, New Mexico in 1947. Despite early reports of a crashed disc, only day

later did the cover up begin with the Army Airforce declaring the debris as a weather balloon.

The UFO phenomenon began after the United States developed the atom bomb and used it against Japan to assist the end of the remainder of the axis forces at the end of WWII. Then, after that, were many sightings all over the world. When more than fifty UFO made a flyover of Washington, DC, in 1952, President Harry S. Truman became quite alarmed at this violation of airspace over the capitol. He wanted answers from the military joint chiefs immediately regarding the threat to national security. He signed the national security act which began the creation of a top-secret group known as the Majestic 12. They were assigned to investigate the military implications and threat to the security of the United States. Their operations and investigations were declared top secret. Officially their investigations fell under the provisions of Project Sign, then Project Grudge and finally Project Bluebook.

Dr. J Allen Hynek was brought in to provide the technical analysis of these sightings, but his real job was to debunk the experiences of witnesses as much as possible to keep the public from peering into military research and development. A more aggressive approach by the military was to shoot down the discs and retrieve them for back engineering research, which was conducted at Groom Lake, a secret Air Force base, commonly known now as Area 51 located in the desert near Reno, Nevada.

With the closure of Project bluebook, the subject of the reality of UFOs was supposedly shut down, however, it was later discovered through the freedoms of information act, the government continued their research through another project called AATIP, Advanced Aerospace threat Identification Program where the designation of a UFO became UAP (Unidentified Arial Phenomenon).

The primary purpose of these organizations was to create a misinformation and deterrent program to persuade the public interest in the phenomenon. However, despite the government declaration that with the close of Project Bluebook defining the end of the government investigations stating there was no real evidence of these sighting to be more than natural phenomenon or mass hysteria has not put an end to the continued private interest, such as MUFON(Mutual UFO Network).

Since the 1990s, Doctor Steven Greer, an emergency room surgeon has taken up the gauntlet to challenge the secrecy and black ops military programs in attempts to subpoena members of the military industrial complex, by spearheading congressional interest in the public release of the UFO phenomenon and subsequent efforts by the military to cover up their crashed UFO retrieval program. He has gathered many willing pilots, military people of high rank as well as astronomers and astrophysicists to join in his efforts to force disclosure by these military operations which are operating outside of the law.

To date, Dr. Greer has little or no success with these efforts. Perhaps he may not realize the depth and breadth of the military exposure of such disclosure. It is known that there are several secret underground bases operated by both human military and alien personnel. A trickle of proof was revealed when a Scottish hacker by the name of Gary McKinnon broke into federal military databases and discovered that under several black ops secret programs, listed both American military personnel as well as several alien officers. Mr. McKinnon is charged with 6 counts of espionage and awaiting extradition from the United Kingdom where he is now living.

During the Eisenhower administration, the president was on a golfing trip to palm springs one weekend and then he disappeared for three days under cloak of secret meetings with foreign dignitaries. In truth he was whisked away to Edwards Air Force base to engage with aliens who offered the US technical help to develop ways and means of improving the life of humans on the earth.

Discussions regarding their help was restricted to medical knowledge and ways to clean up waste in the water and in the air. When the military attaché suggested military assistance, the aliens refused. In that meeting, they warned the president and the other military personnel should they get an offer of assistance from the Grays of the Zeta Reticula star system, it would not serve them because the Zetas are known to be hostile toward humans and they have their own agend as toward humans in the future.

The Pleiadeans left and the Zetas arrived later. The US agreed to provide numbers of humans to the alien bases for their own scientific analysis of humans in exchange for military weapons development. Since the government could not decipher the alien technology, from crashed UFOs, the aliens offered their assistance which is why the US military has raced ahead with super weapons and new energy sources.

That technology boost also comes in the form of the transistor development, laser development, integrate circuitry and the development of microprocessors which advanced communication drastically resulting in our cell phone usage. Fiber optics, and quantum computing have emerged from this exchange. Perhaps the Pleiadean's warning has yet to manifest but they may be playing a strong role in the ultimate domination of the prison here.

The government has been busy building Deep Underground Military bases for years. The estimated number of these bases is about 103, spread across the United States and connected by monorail as well as highways wide enough to allow two semi-trailer trucks to travel side by side.

There are about 1,000,000 people who disappear annually around the world without a trace, a tenth of that from the US alone. The shocking truth is our government is doing most of the abductions over the years, apart from the occasional abduction by other species coming here.

## Secret Deals to be Made

Just about all reports of flying saucers stem from the Roswell, New Mexico crash incident, first reported as it truly was. Then days later, modified by the United States Army Air Core to be a weather balloon, the first public example of a coverup.

In truth, the incidents of extraterrestrial visitation go back in history for tens if not hundreds-of thousands of years, illustrated by many different cultures and civilizations around the world described in the Indian work the Mahabarata, part of the ancient Rig Vedas (meaning truthful history). Also, a 450,000-year history of the settlement of an extraterrestrial race of beings in the Mesopotamia region near the Tigress and Euphrates rivers basin as recorded by the ancient Sumerian cuneiform clay tablets, dating back 10,000 years, found under the ruins of the city of Ninevah temples as examples.

In 1952, UFO swarms were sighted flying over the Capitol for several days causing President Truman to create a task force to investigate the serious nature of this violation of airspace and potential military threat to the security of the United States. This task force was called Majestic Twelve, a group of high-ranking military personnel and top industrial corporate leaders. They were given the highest Top-Secret clearance of 'Majestic'. All reports of sightings would be filtered through and investigated as to their authenticity and threat evaluation and reported to the president.

Since that time to the present, several government projects were created under the jurisdiction of Majestic Twelve authority: Beginning with the Roswell UFO incident; The Bookings report; The Condon Committee; Estimate of the Situation; Project Blue Book; Project Grudge; Project Serpo; Project Sign; Project Silver Bug; The Robertson Panel; The All-Domain Anomaly Resolution Office(AARO); NASA's UAP Independent Study Team; The Unidentified Anomalous Phenomena Disclosure Act and the most recent; The Advanced Aerospace Threat Identification Program(AATIP). Since the release of Project Bluebook, headed up by Dr. J. Allen Hynek as physicist and scientific consultant, the first director was Air Force Captain Edward J. Ruppelt, then after Lieutenant Colonel Hector Quintanilla who became the chief officer before the program was terminated December 17, 1969, though some would say the last day of activity was January 30, 1970.

The official position of the United Staes Air Force was no evidence could be found in the thousands of reports of these phenomenon other than normal explanations of natural events and or mistaken observations. No official acknowledgement of any government activity and investigations had been siteduntil December 2017. Leaked disclosure of a secret project that studied UFOs and unexplained aerial phenomena (UAP) from 2007 to 2012. Then another program was revealed before congress by whistle blowers in addition to the AATIP Program, described as a secret crash retrieval program operated by the military industrial complex.

McDonnel Douglas, Sperry Rand, Lockheed-Martin Skunk Works, Martin-Marietta and North American Rocketdyne Corporations to name a few, were involved in these secret programs, considered as 'black ops' with trillion dollar budgets without oversight, to recover crashed UFOs and occupants and brought to Wright-Patterson Air Force and White Sands Testing grounds at Alamogordo, and Los Alamos Laboratories in New

Mexico for analysis and possible back engineering. This was a process where existing alien craft would be duplicated for the use by the military as part of the secret United States arsenal of weapons.

There is evidence that in the spring of 1953, President Dwight D. Eisenhower traveled to Palm Springs for a weekend of golf. But he officially disappeared during that time for three days. He was secretly whisked away to Wright-Patterson Air Force base for a secret meeting with extraterrestrials beings called 'tall whites' from the Pleiades star system. They came to offer technological help with our ecological problems of air and water contamination, assistance with agricultural food production and advanced medical knowledge as well as, recommendations for ceasing atomic testing of nuclear weapons as part of their bargain. The president was accompanied by several members of the military joint chiefs providing security as well as advice and counsel.

The Pleiadeans told the president that other races from the Zeta Reticula star system known as the 'Grays' were also coming to bargain with them to discuss similar arrangements. The Grays are only

## Secret Deals to be Made

3-4 feet tall in stature more closely compared to science fiction movies in Hollywood as 'little green men'!

The military wanted advanced knowledge of propulsion and weapon technology to be on the bargaining table, but the Pleiadeans refused. Before they left, they warned that the Grays had other agendas with their desire to bargain and were not having our best interests in mind.

Shortly thereafter, the Zeta Grays from Reticula arrived and made similar offers but already knowing the military mind set of the government, cut to the chase and offered all their technology including propulsion systems, advanced weaponry such as powerful lasers and microcomputer systems, advanced metallurgy techniques with new alloys, particle beam technology and telecommunication systems.

The agenda for the grays involved the desire to experiment on human subjects. They wanted to abduct at least one million subjects a year including male, female and children and required their own secret bases to be built with joint military operations to facilitate training in under water and underground facilities on earth.

The government agreed with the caveat that the abductees would not remember anything of their experiences. The aliens said no problem!

According to the United States Census Bureau, at least one million people disappear every year without a trace. The sad part of this story is it is the Military carrying out the abductions with alien reconstruction vehicles, not the aliens for the most part.

In 1955 Area 51 opened and was established as part of the Nevada test and training range. A survey team arrived on May 4th at Groom Lake and laid out a runway where an older airfield already existed but had not been used since World War II. The CIA selected this remote site to test the U-2 spy plane. The base was originally called the 'ranch' consisting of shelters, workshops and tailer homes.

The new strip was to be a 5,000-foot North-South facing runway at the southwest corner of the ranch. The CIA, Air Force and Lockheed, later known only as Skunk Works arrived in July of that year. The U-2 was put into service in 1956. Area 51 was the home of the A-12 reconnaissance plane, the F-117 stealth fighter, the B-2 stealth bomber, the Blackbird and various designs of ARVs (Alien Reconstruction Vehicles) that use augmented anti-gravity propulsion.

One example is the TR3-B craft which is triangular shaped and can travel much more than many times the speed of sound or greater and exhibit flight characteristics normally attributed to alien craft. Without control surfaces and obvious propulsion artifacts such as the exhaust of burned jet fuel, were often mistaken as UFOs seen by observers. Area 51 is highly classified and protected from unauthorized entry by patrolled military personnel. Workers are brought to the base by special air transport from Las Vegas airport and bussed to and from the base each day.

One example of a secret underground base operated by American military and alien scientists is known by Hopi indigenous peoples in the area to be at an undisclosed location near the Archuleta Archipelago near Dulce, New Mexico.

Dr. Steven Greer, a retired ER surgeon, has been working with members of the military as well as members of congress since 1991 to achieve a full public disclosure of the government coverup and involvement with the existing alien presence on earth. He has had little or no success with this mission.

After seeing video taken aboard the orbiting shuttle shown live to the public, accidentally revealed many lights moving at great speeds along the surface of the earth. At one moment, one light moving very fast in a straight line made a sudden right-angled maneuver, demonstrating its ability to avoid serious inertial changes to the occupants, moved with anticipated advance of a sudden beam of light (obviously, to me seemed to be an activated particle beam) shot from the earth surface at the UFO, designed to take down the vehicle. It was a near miss. Perhaps then, in truth all the crashes in the past may not be due to vehicular mishaps but our military using advanced weaponry given to them to attack these alien ships, to further their collection of technological artifacts.

## Soul Collector Vortex

There are many untruths perpetrated by religious dogma regarding the soul. The first is the idea that the soul is in mortal danger of destruction through damnation. This idea is a religious mechanism of psychological manipulation to impose control and subjugation of the masses through fear of retribution and punishment from God. This manipulation is not relegated only to Christian concepts. In Eastern religious dogma there is the idea of Karma.

The idea of 'bad' karma is utilized to hang over the faithful as a watchdog to keep them from behaving badly by the threat that whatever is done will haunt them with something bad that will happen either later in this life, or in the next. Hence, why the priesthood declares that the soul needs to be saved from the ravages of sin thus proclaiming their important role as saviors of humanity.

To understand and grasp why this is fundamentally untrue is to begin to understand the true value of the human being. Further, it is interesting to note, based on modern alien abduction accounts, that the soul is even coveted by other advanced civilizations on other worlds. We as humans need to wake up to the truth about the true essence of soul.

One of the reasons for expelling the heretical gospels was because within those texts it clearly states that there is no need for an interceder between the faithful and the Highest God. A fact that essentially puts the priesthood out of business.

According to the Sumer historical accounts, when the Anunnaki demigods came to earth, they landed and settled in the Mesopotamian region 450,000 years ago with a purpose to mine for gold. Their home planet, Nibiru, was suffering an atmospheric depletion. They needed powdered gold to keep the atmosphere from slipping away. Their workers, the Iggigi, began extracting gold from the Euphrates River, but it was not enough to supply their needs. They realized they would need to mine the larger deposits from the earth and that work was far more difficult and the Iggigi refused. The Anunnaki Genetic engineers, Enki, and Isis, sought to find an appropriate indigenous life form in the area, strong enough and advanced enough that only minor genetic alterations would provide a good mining work force intelligent enough to understand their commands, smart enough to operate their equipment but not smart enough to rebel against their overlords. Isis determined that the bipedal Hominid known as Homo-Erectus would be a perfect specimen.

The average life span in the normal evolution of the humanoids (the hominids) was more than a thousand years. Time needed to accomplish all this genetic work was of the essence. The Anunnaki overlord, King Anu, demanded to create a work force immediately to mine the gold and return it to Nibiru, as their planet's atmosphere was failing fast. A speedy solution was needed. The first order of genetic business was to shorten the hominid's life span.

Many DNA alterations were needed. The test results of each cycle needed to be quick to realize successful results. The Anunnaki engineers Enki and Isis, shortened the hominid's life span to three score and ten years (roughly 70 years). This allowed confirmation that the DNA alterations were effective. After the changes were made Isis discovered that the new hybrids could not reproduce. She realized the individual manipulation of each Homo-Erectus would not supply the demand for a larger work force in time allotted.

The DNA changes altered the Homo-Erectus into Homo-Sapiens. The Anunnaki called the first Homo-Sapiens Adamu, meaning the first Adam. In genesis, the Hebrew scripture of the Israelite's translation of the Sumer historical creation accounts, said God (meaning Jehovah or Yahweh) created Adam in his own image. In the Sumer accounts it was Elohim (those on high or Anunnaki demigods) that created the first Adamu slave. So, when the Hebrew scripture said that God created man in his own image, it was the Elohim, that created Adamu in their image, using altered Hominid DNA with their DNA image.

As a point of Sumer record, Jehovah was an Anunnaki general left behind to rule over the hybrids and continue the mining of gold without interruption until King Anu ordered the complete destruction of the Adamites by virtue of a flood.

Despite King Anu's command to limit the abilities of the hybrids, Enki decided to add his own DNA to the mix making it possible for the hybrids to procreate, and they did in greater numbers. However, this also increased the evolutionary possibility for Homo-Sapiens to become more powerful like the demi-gods.

The fundamental DNA of the Anunnaki was reptilian in essence. Here again, is another misinterpretation of the Sumer accounts in the Hebrew scripture, which tells the story of the snake (the reptilian in the garden of Edan) tempting Eve, the companion of Adam. But the Hebrew account describes the forbidden fruit (the apple) of the tree of life (as knowledge of good and evil) which is a description of the Vegas Nerve complex in the brain. King Anu forbade the Adamu to be able to procreate for fear that they would multiply and become smart enough to rebel.

So, it was Enki, the reptilian, who tempted Isis (Eve) to make the addition of his DNA to alter the nerve complex (the tree of life inside the Homo-Sapiens brain) offering the Adamites procreative ability. This change offered greater knowledge and evolution for all the Adamites as well. King Anu became angry and cast out all Adamites from the Anunnaki home Ship, called Ehdan, meaning a garden.

From the spiritual perspective, the Highest God

acting out of the highest heavenly realm, the quantum, wanted to correct the effect of this evolutionary change brought about by the Anunnaki. The single lifetime was replaced by multiple lifetimes as a system of reincarnation. Many lifetimes could be utilized to gather experience in which to develop awareness and wisdom. With time, many incarnations could provide enough experience and insight making possible the convergence of that experience and the emergence of a new self-awareness. This self-awareness is called a soul. The evolution of the soul through continued learning and self-discovery could lead to the ultimate loss of the ego and the defiance of the spirit that caused the original 'sin' or fall from heaven (the loss of self-consciousness). Increased self-awareness could conceivably offer the recovery of the lost memories with a subsequent return to grace.

The counterpoint against the benefit of reincarnating is the chance to repeat mistakes because there is significant memory loss of experience during the birthing process. The process of leaving one life and entering another is starting over as an infant. It would be ideal if one could continue where, one left off. In that way, a continuous life could occur with intermittent breaks. As an infant, the new creation of another body and mind, loses everything from the previous life. This means no memory of anything from the past is brought forward into the new mind and body.

So, the real possibility arises that mistakes made in the past life are quite easily repeated if the initial behavior carries over. The alteration of previous behavior could not occur necessarily since lessons learned will not be remembered. This aspect becomes a double edge sword so to speak. Bad experiences can be put behind with a fresh start in theory, which is a good thing. However, it is also likely that certain traits may crop up again offering the individual choices that may go either way and the likelihood of making the same choices are statistically high.

The other contributory factor added to the process is that the next life has the probability of being like the past life due to inherent traits emerging within the DNA as stored predilections. These can make an impression on the life force which can predetermine the arrangement of similar life circumstances going forward. In addition, the system of life repeating in this cycle of birth and death then is very much like a hamster wheel. The individual is stuck repeating the same patterns ad infinitum. Also, there is the influence of the DNA of both parents contributing to the repeating issues. The truth is that reincarnation occurs mostly within family groups where issues are adapted by swapping perspectives from one familial sibling to another giving the opportunity to gain insight and or wisdom regarding the individual issues that arise between each. Also, this exchange can occur between the parents and children in some cases.

In its essence, this plan seemed to be a good solution to the shortened life span as far as development is concerned. These flaws with this system then make the likelihood of development taking an extremely long time, perhaps hundreds, if not thousands of lifetimes, to correct behaviors while adjusting the understanding of these situations to move on to higher existence. Since the quantum has no time, meaning all events happen at the same time, how long it took to make changes didn't matter because time in the physical is just part of the illusion here.

That said, unfortunately, this system of incarnation has been hacked so to speak. The promise of living a good life with the hope of moving into paradise as a reward of good behavior, after slogging through the slings and arrows of misfortunate in the physical, a belief that is quite common amongst people. Once again, this promise is perpetrated by religious doctrines and their dogmatic teachings, while the truth of life repeating here is not present in the consciousness and kept secret as a myth from the masses.

When I say the system has been hacked, I'm referring to other extraterrestrial forces (not Anunnaki) that are also reptilian but are Draconian in their nature, not benign and are ruling this planet. For this reason, the author declares this planet as a slave planet. Those living here are unaware that they are unconscious prisoners of the 'new' overlords that secretly rule through many human groups governing the masses through alien mind control. As Gurdjieff, a Russian philosopher and spiritual teacher once said, "we are food for the moon". It turns out that our moon is an artificial satellite that is a monitoring station and a source for the alien mind control signal from these Draconian reptilians. Though this idea sounds utterly like science fiction, the truth of this was revealed with the moon expeditions in the early 70's. Experiments to drop the lunar lander take-off booster back to the moon's surface to shake the moon caused it to ring like a bell for hours suggesting to NASA that the moon is hollow!

Those who are aware of this alien influence and control and behind the agreements with those aliens to provide human subjects for alien experimentation are given alien technology for advanced transportation and weaponry and are paid handsomely, enjoying the fruits of powerful positions within the hierarchy of government. They have made their pact with the 'devil' so to speak. They care not for their own future beyond what is given to them, in exchange for their betrayal of their fellow man. It is sad and unfortunate for the rest of humanity as they carry on with the coverup of this dark conspiracy.

They have abandoned the pursuit of evolution to a higher purpose in life for the existential benefits of the present 'reality'. In other words, they have become the guards of the prison and watch that everyone stays in line and will offer rebellious specimens or kill those who don't.

This idea may sound preposterous to many people and certainly as a fellow human being, writing about this easily places this author into the category of a deranged unhinged whistle blower who has lost all his mental capacities and rational perspectives. However, there are many learned and highly educated people who have been involved and or discovered this truth and have tried to reveal it. Not all have lived to tell the tale so to speak. These facts remain behind the veil of the government's above top-secret security.

The media outlets including the social media are controlled by giant corporate structures. Large scale misinformation programs are well entrenched in our social and government settings by law enforcement and intelligence organizations representing the military industrial complex for decades now, since the end of the second World War. President Eisenhower offered a warning to the public about the dangers posed by the military industrial complex implying its status as an unchecked secret government or deep state well-funded without oversight in his farewell speech on January 17th, 1961.

Intelligent extraterrestrial civilizations are out there and are also living here among the populace, in some cases in plain sight. Honest God-fearing people see the evidence before them every day, but they are continuously humiliated to the point that they no longer believe their own eyes and ears and sheepishly accept what they see and have been told.

Many technologists agree that the advance of technology over the last 79 years constitutes a giant leap of progress. Even before the second world war ended, the German engineering developed jet powered aircraft, ballistic missiles, anti-gravity craft called Hanabu.

After the war, the United States offered immunity for war crimes to 1100 German scientists to come to America to become part of NASA to help American efforts to compete with Soviets in the post-war space-race. Werner Von Braun who led the development of the Jupiter C rocket that put American astronauts on the moon, was asked later how the Germans developed their science and technology so quickly. Werner said, "we had help from extraterrestrials".

In America, the sudden advance of technology has also continued to completely outstrip the normal scale attributed to natural scientific progression such as Fiber optics, the microcomputer chip, aerial craft traveling at 10 times the speed of sound, radar and radar resistant designs, geosynchronous satellites circling the earth providing guidance and location information to automobiles and cell phones just to name a few.

Look for example, at the impact of ripping the old telephones off the walls and from the common telephone booths in the act of progress, then putting a minicomputer (cell phone) into the hands of almost everyone on the planet to facilitate greater communications. Seems like a great advance in human progress, right? Yet, no one has admitted to the dangerous effects of very high frequency electromagnetic energy broadcasting to cell towers and at the same time broadcasting that same powerful and dangerous signal to the brains of the public! Case in point, just try to obtain a copy of a secret internal study developed by Nokia regarding the details of this radiation danger!

People are not communicating with each other now, face to face. Instead, they have an augmented device to do it for them anytime they want. But these devices are, in truth, seductive and less a telephone and more of a listening tool for those who wish to know where you are, what you are doing, thinking, and most of all what you want and are willing to buy from the corporations, especially things you don't need all for the sake of keeping up the economy. So, in the author's opinion, this so-called advanced technology has served to eliminate close quarter contact and is separating people, even young children.

Now the social platforms such as Twitter, Facebook and Ticktock are used to program the thinking of adults and children alike through misinformation and false flags. This keeps them from gathering into groups and forming separate opinions and ideas because the elite know that groups are inherently more powerful than individuals.

This author wishes to add a small ray of light and

love within the purpose and point of this treatise. This author is not trying to undermine or overthrow any faction here, but to extend a hopeful message to wake up, appealing to the inner most thread of every human on the planet. Being a prisoner is not great but being unconscious about it is worse in the author's opinion and can institute change.

So, with that said, the author is expanding on the idea that the true heart of the human, even with all the inherent flaws, still stands out and above the dehumanizing effect of activities of transhuman advocators that would choose artificial intelligence added to their construct while at the same time, undermining self-confidence and destroying real hope of a better existence by usurping the authentic importance and opportunities to advance and grow into greater beings of higher consciousness organically.

Before I completely overwhelm the reader of the seriousness of the impact and insidious nature of the darkness enveloping the planet, I will now move onto other points of this treatise.

As astounding as it may seem, the idea that the soul can be quantized, categorized and tabulated like a digital piece of data, though well beyond our capability and conceptualization, is well within the technological capability of the Chi Ahkar reptilian alien race.

This device will be described in rough terms. I do not understand this kind of biological technology to adequately define it inner working principles. That said, it is my understanding in very general terms, that it does exist and is being used now on earth extending from our nearest artificial satellite called the moon, where such a device does exist and is being used to literally collect souls.

Though there is some hardware involved to create this collection and storage of energetic spiritual essence. The location of this equipment is located on the dark side of the moon, placed in one of the larger craters that are positioned near the edge of the tidal lock perimeter, nearly in view of the earth but cloaked within an energy field that masks its presence. The energetic aspects are like the time-space loop used to keep the earth locked within an artificial matrix of physical reality well beyond our ability to detect it. That will be the subject of a later chapter.

## Soul Collector Vortex

As one considers this amazing aspect of Chi Ahkar technology, you are left with many questions, such as why would they want to store a soul? Are they using that energy for a kind of organic energy like a battery or just to study it beyond the influence or obstruction of the physical body? It turns out that they are performing experiments that are even more astounding, that would confront human imagination.

They are cloning humanoid bodies, not necessarily precisely human, as an exact replica but modified hybrid clones(a mix of reptilian and human DNA) to represent a form that would allow surface accommodations but keeping some of their traits they need to continue their own consciousness. Moreover, why would they not want to keep their own consciousness stacked as it were, to implant into these cloned physical structures? The simple answer to this is that human consciousness is interlinked to the human form DNA immune system.

A long-standing agenda by the Dracos on earth, is their confinement to their underground domiciles and facilities in favor of returning to the surface like they are in the Orion system. Their home world is considerably more distant from the sequence star, so surface dwelling is not a problem there. On earth is another story.

Here the earth is third planet from the sun with its orbital path only 93,000,000 miles distant. The Dracos are very sensitive to light despite a second eyelid that can shield them from sudden bursts of strong light, but on earth this would require their second lid to be closed for most of the time while above ground on the surface, which cuts down the vision of their surrounding environment considerably. This problem is also exacerbated by the instability of solar radiation of a young star that often arises, especially during a solar maximum period (the near end of an eleven-year cycle) when sunspot and solar flares as well as coronal mass ejections can be prevalent.

That stands as the main comparison between Betelgeuse (their main sequence star) which is a solar orb that is older and already passed on from its yellow light phase to its redlight phase of life. This means it is cooler and not as bright. The caveat to this is Betelgeuse is nearer to a nova (the complete collapse of the star) resulting in a white dwarf condition. As a red star, it does not go through sunspots flares, CMEs and coronal hole ejection of protons. This fact may be the reason the Chi Ahkar seek other star systems to migrate to and consume, bringing them into their ever-growing empire. Their choices of other star systems take in the existing condition of other systems' stars and their age for this reason.

Our sun, known as Sol, is a young star which has not entered the second phase of expansion to the red light radiation level. However, because the earth is in the third orbit of the system, when Sol does expand, it will alter what our astrophysicists call the goldilocks zone of perfect life conditions. In the expansion of the sun into a red light phase will encroach upon the zone of the third orbit and would consume the earth which eliminates earth as a habitable planet in the long term. That represents another problem overshadowing their occupation of earth as a more immediate consideration.

So, the sun's reduction to a white dwarf resulting from helium depletion and thus gravitational collapse into a white dwarf is perhaps some millions-of-years into the future. Whereas in the moment, the Dracos need to stay out of harm's way below ground. The exposure to X-rays, Gamma rays, and high-speed proton radiation from coronal holes could be lethal to them on the surface. Creating hybrid clones containing human DNA as well as Chi Ahkar DNA would require a soul present to drive the organic mechanism properly.

One additional issue would be the subconscious memory of human experience remaining as a residue from previous incarnations. That could interfere with Chi Ahkar intentions. This problem is handled by mind-wiping. A technique used as an off chute of mind control technology, only in this case, it strips previous influences of past life experiences and emotional components which might subject their potential interference and disrupt reptilian mental acuity and the reptilian force of will. A presence of emotional energy residue would be undesirable in a militaristic civilization.

The decision to invade this solar system became a strategic move that overrode other components relating to their immediate living conditions here. Ultimately their intention is to extract the minerals while here and make use of the value of human DNA as well as the soul components which may be useful in the invasion of similar systems in the future. In the meantime, they have claimed earth as their own and will not leave willingly until they are done here.

In the United States and other countries around the world, the concept of reincarnation is not generally accepted as part of the modern Christian religious doctrine. This doctrine is divided into several denominations, including Catholicism, Protestantism and the Eastern Orthodox Church. Protestantism includes many traditions, such as Anglicanism, Baptists, Lutheranism, Methodism and Pentecostalism. The concept of reincarnation spoken of in the Gnostic Gospels may have been removed by Constantine at the Counsel of Mycenae where most of the Gnostic Gospels were expelled and declared heretical.

The Eastern Orthodox Church is a communion of independent churches that recognize each other and is the second-largest Christian body in the world. In Greece, the Orthodox Church does not recognize Jesus as a divine being but rather a great prophet.

The Catholic Church is a communion of churches that includes 23 Eastern churches. The core Protestant doctrinal belief is The Trinity, a belief that God is one being as three components, the father, the son and the holy ghost. The person of Jesus Christ is both fully human and fully divine.

There is also included in this doctrine of the Second Coming, which states that Jesus will return to the earth heralding the beginning of his reign upon earth for a millennium. The primary structural differences between Catholic tradition and Protestant denominations are the priesthood.

The clerical system in Protestantism has Deacons or Preachers in place of priests. One exception is the Lutheran denomination which is closest in structure to the Catholic form. The other specific exception is with the Baptist denomination that requires the submergence into water as a confirmation of faith, reflecting the practice stemming from John the Baptist, having dunked followers into the river Jordan preceding the appearance of Jesus on the scene.

After Jesus' crucifixion and purported resurrection, the spread of this doctrine carried through to other Middle Eastern countries beyond Israel by way of Jesus' disciples, who came to be known as the Apostles of Christ, spreading the word of his gospel. This included Greece, Turkey, and Persia which is now Iraq and Iran. The intermixing and strong influx of the Gnostic traditions of Eastern

Mysticism into Christian doctrine stemmed from the early Christian principles established by the Essene Brotherhood and the mystical school at Mount Carmel led by the prophet Elijah, by way of the constant flow of caravans, which included Mary Magdalene, whose father managed several of those caravans.

Jesus was considered a Nazarene yet the euphemism of his origin as a place called Nazareth is a myth. The sect of Nazarenes was related to the Essene brotherhood that lived in an enclave outside of Jerusalem near Mount Carmel. Mystical rituals and secret gnostic beliefs and practices included the concept of reincarnation. It is believed that this doctrine was brought into Gnostic doctrine by way of the religious knowledge of India.

India is the origin of Buddhism, Hinduism and Islam. In Buddhism the supreme being is Brahman, the God force present in all things. This doctrine included Karma, where good deeds lead to positive outcomes, while harmful actions lead to negative consequences. Moksha represents the highest goal of human life, which can be achieved through Yoga and meditation. Also included, Dharma is the concept of duty, righteousness and moral order.

Buddhism, stemming from the teachings of Mahatma Siddhartha Buddha, is defined by Dukkha, a life that leads to suffering, Kama where desire is the root cause of suffering and Bodhi as enlightenment, the liberated state that can be achieved by giving up desire and following the eight-fold path of Yoga.

In Hinduism, there are many Gods which include Vishnu and Shiva. So, reincarnation is the system where the Soul's Sojourn would include death and rebirth many times based upon previous life behavior until Bodhi is achieved.

Another offshoot of this doctrine is mixed in and often misunderstood as equal to reincarnation which is Transmigration. In this case, incarnations begin with lower animal life and eventually migrate into the higher form which is human. In this doctrine includes a kind of Karmic retribution that relates to morality, depending on negative behavior a soul could migrate backward into animal form again as a kind of Karmic punishment.

The Prime Mover or Origin Source originally devised the system of reincarnation to provide a way for the fallen to return to the Godhead. Their original essence before the fall was as a hermaphrodite (polarity of both Male and female combined). The betrayer separated the soul's substance, then broken, separated it into male and female essence, and then reintroduced it into their animal hosts. This tricked the souls already in a fallen condition, were no longer able to ascend back into heaven.

The source blamed the betrayer for this horrible transgression. Full of anger and spite he intended that the fallen would never return to source and deceived the souls to believe that engaging in copulation and procreation would provide the encouragement and example of union. However, the copulation and birth of the offspring of the animal hosts, captured a percentage of their soul essence dividing it and infusing only a part into the offspring.

Thus, with each copulation and procreation their essence was further divided ultimately into nothingness. A complete and utter isolation from source resulted. They forgot who they were. The process of Reincarnation would have become the solution to the awful condition established by the cruelty of the betrayer. This idea provided the only way of salvation of the fallen souls from the complete oblivion of unconsciousness. Through many lifetimes it was hoped that the lost and divided souls would come to eventually awaken and remember. The lost connection and subsequent loss of awareness and separation from Source, together with a misunderstanding of translated scripture, gave rise to the origin and the concept of sex being at the heart of original sin by religious scholars today.

The Chi Ahkar slavers being the offspring of the betrayer, sought to enslave mankind upon the earth by usurping this process of reincarnation for their own ends. They realized that this reincarnation process would lead the way to breaking out of their prison. So, the Chi Ahkar reconfigured their mind control transmitter-receivers on the artificial satellite to capture the mental imagery of the human consciousness as they are passing out of the animal body, copying the familial reflections of family members which have already passed on. Then the regenerated 3D projected holograms of these familial patterns into the 4D energy field reflecting the warmth and acceptance of these souls, as they were remembered, to influence and persuade the souls leaving their bodies.

The slave masters then used these fake projections to cause the souls passing, to enter the 'tunnel' of light, the portal mechanism which channels them back into the 3D earth realm, like a black hole, sucking them back into the prison matrix where their essence and feelings would be stored and continue to feed the Chi Ahkar addiction and delight. In this way, the natural evolution afforded to the passing soul by virtue of the reincarnation process would be interrupted and brought into a continuous loop of illusion, the earth prison. This is the eternal 'hamster wheel' secret that no one knows about. Once the soul enters that channel of light, a laser-like corridor, there is no turning back.

The only way out of this nightmare is to refuse the seduction of these fake holograms beckoning the soul to enter the light. Only by refusing this action can the soul separate but it must endure the void for a time until beings of the Galactic Federation of Worlds can capture the soul and begin their re-education and continued evolution as the Prime Mover had intended.

So, there are soul catchers that sit at the periphery of each spiritual event horizon hoping to catch the soul before it is tricked into the false support of the soul trap. This rejection at the critical moment of separation from the body will require courage and faith that this is the truth. Unfortunately, this dire condition is almost like an aphrodisiac to the soul. The catchers cannot interfere until the soul chooses to exit the trap of its own free will.

The subject of alien abductions is controversial at best. Perhaps the locales where these incidents occur would best be described as remote and relatively unpopulated zones. More than a million people disappear per year according to the US Bureau of Statistics. In the continental United States, areas that report the highest percentage of disappearances of people are beginning with Alaska. Nome is first because the only way into Nome is by air because of the rugged terrain, roads are not possible or even existing. Second is Oklahoma, having the largest percentage of missing people in America, with Louisiana and Arkansas also above average based upon the latest federal statistics. The data also points to wide regional variations, with the southern states having some of the highest percentages of missing people. Sri Lanka is also listed internationally as well as Native American and Alaskan indigenous communities.

Though in some of the particular circumstances may range from subsequent murders related to disappearances where the bodies of the victims are not found immediately, or many years go by with files that become 'cold case' where the investigations are dropped and local law enforcement yield to the denial of the additional expense of manpower and investigative services to any further continuation of investigations and the importance of relative additional work loads.

Many circumstances arising from reported missing persons may also be related to domestic violence or domestic disputes where the spouse (either male or female) may report such an incident. Here in this case, most state authorities will not even pursue an investigation until after 3 days have passed because in those cases, the parties that have gone missing will return within that period.

Some cases of campers or members of hiking groups may get lost in the wilderness and though search parties are implemented, the zones of wilderness
That involve mountainous or rugged terrain, may preclude the use of search and rescue helicopters besides ground search parties directed by forestry rangers will abandon searches after several days of sweeping the last-known whereabouts of those people reported missing. It would be assumed that those individuals have been severely injured by a

fall, fallen unconscious and or death by predators and dragged off into their respective lairs.

Another famous abduction case of Betty and Barney Hill, an interracial couple that lost three hours on a New Hampshire highway on their way home on the night of September 19, 1961. The story of their experience would become the first truly credible story of an alien encounter. Driving south on route 3 through the white mountains, the saw a light in the sky sometime after 10 p.m. They followed it for a while, stopping to get a better look. They continued driving getting home around 5 a.m. They commented later that the trip should have been only 3 hours arriving no later than 2 a.m. Reluctant to talk about it, eventually the Hills underwent hypnosis with the aid of psychiatrist Benjamin Simon which revealed that at some point along their trip they came into contact and taken aboard an alien spaceship.

They had been separately probed and examined by the alien visitors before. Being released. Betty also revealed she had a conversation with the captain of the craft and asked him where they were from. he brought her over to a star map and revealed a cluster of stars indicating trade routes. She was able under the hypnotic trance to redraw what she saw. Later her drawing matched very precisely the star cluster now known as the Zeta Reticula system in greater detail.

## Implants, Alien Tracers

The idea that aliens could come to you in the middle of the night and inject foreign objects into your body, smacks of a thriller sci-fi movie or in a more shocking case that you are on a quiet road sometime walking along minding your own business and suddenly a flying saucer unexpectedly swoops down, scoops you up and takes you into a room on board and proceeds to violate every orifice, while at the same time, taking DNA samples is nightmarish.

Then they have the audacity to leave implanted in your body, a foreign object that is shoved up your nose or embedded behind the ear or some other location which constitutes an advanced form of micro-transmitter sending out signals identifying you and your precise location. This would be needed for the sole purpose of hunting you down later for yet another round of examinations at their discretion, is simply outrageous.

Perhaps in your mind, there comes the thought that, is this not against all the rules and regulations of interplanetary protocol! Who would you complain to in that case? Well, this seems to be the case in quite a few cases of abductions.

If you do tell someone, then you are ridiculed and humiliated, labeled a lunatic ready for the men to arrive with a white jacket suited just for you. But wait, some of these implants are not always compatible to the human organism. In the case of those that are placed high up inside the nasal passage often becomes quite irritating and causes nose bleeds. Until that happens, you may never know you have one of these objects. In fact, its those who eventually arrive at their doctor's office to report a sudden and unexplained continuous nosebleed that reveals the alien treachery!

An implant would be the last thought entering a physician's mind but after a bit of probing and prodding and a tiny little metal piece comes out laid carefully onto a tissue, staring at you and the good doctor of its improbable existence squarely confronting both of you with a healthy dose of incredulity leaving you to question temporary insanity.

In the main the idea that people are receiving implants is still out there in mainstream science. In most cases, the doctor will find something, he will label some debris and simply remove and toss the artifact into the waste can without even examining it closely. He or she may then say well, odd that you managed to inhale a foreign object. The good news is they got it out for you, end of story.

A surgeon by the name of Roger K. Leir has published a book called "Aliens and the Scalpel", the personal story behind the greatest breakthrough of all time-scientific proof that anomalous bio-electromagnetic implants of extraterrestrial origin have been removed from persons reporting alien abduction experiences. He has also published a second volume, Casebook: Alien Implants. Dr. Leir has had these objects analyzed in the top laboratories in the country establishing the material are made of metal alloys that do not exist on earth. Further, that these miniature pieces of high technology emit frequencies and magnetic fields without any obvious way to power them.

Sometimes the objects are large enough to notice as lumps under the skin or mounted next to major bones and show up when X-rays are taken of the area. Some items are mounted under the gums or inside a tooth that has had a root canal. Another popular location is behind the ear and a small X shaped scar is evidence that something has been added.

Sometimes the implants will cause an irritation below the skin and become very itchy. Sometimes the implants will cause a dull ache near a bone joint and be analyzed to be a simple case of neuralgia or arthro-arthritis. In each of these cases the item is buried deep enough that surgery is the only solution for removal.

The following is taken from a WikiLeaks's transcript of the written testimony of Luis Elizondo for the U.S. House Committee on Oversight and Accountability Subcommittees on Cybersecurity, Information Technology, and Government Innovation and National Security, the Border, and Foreign Affairs. Unidentified Anomalous Phenomena: Exposing the Truth Wednesday, November 13, 2024.

Greetings, Chairwoman Mace, Chairman Grothman, Ranking Members Connolly and Garcia, and Members of the Committee. It is my honor and privilege to testify before you on the issue of unidentified anomalous phenomena, formerly known as UFOs. On behalf of the brave men and women in uniform and across the intelligence community, as well as my fellow Americans who have waited for this day, thank you for your leadership on this important matter.

Let me be clear: UAP are real. Advanced technologies not made by our government, or any other government are monitoring sensitive military installations around the globe. Furthermore, the U.S.

is in possession of UAP technologies, as are some of our adversaries. I believe we are in a multi-decade, secretive arms race, one funded by misallocated taxpayer dollars and hidden from elected representatives and oversight bodies.

For many years, I was entrusted with protecting some of our nation's most sensitive programs. In my last position, I managed a Special Access Program on behalf of the White House and the National Security Council. As such, I appreciate the need to protect certain sensitive intelligence and military information. I consider my oath to protect secrets as sacred and will always put the safety of the American people first. With that said, I also understand the consequences of excessive secrecy and stove-piping. Nowhere was this more apparent than in the aftermath of 9/11, which many of us remember all too well. I believe that America's greatness depends on three elements:
- a watchful Congress
- a responsive Executive Branch
- an informed public.

Over the last decade and a half, I learned that certain UAP programs were, and are, operating without any of these elements.

Although much of my government work on the UAP subject still remains classified, excessive secrecy has led to grave misdeeds against loyal civil servants, military personnel, and the public. This was to hide the fact that we are not alone in the cosmos.

A small cadre within our own Government involved in the UAP topic has created a culture of suppression and intimidation that I have been victim to, along with many of my former colleagues. This includes unwarranted criminal investigations, harassment, and efforts to destroy one's credibility.

Most Americans would be shocked to learn that the Pentagon's very own Public Affairs Office openly employs a professional psychological operations officer as the singular point of contact for any UAP related inquiries from citizens and the media. This is unacceptable.

Many of my former colleagues and I have provided classified testimony to both the Department of Defense and the Intelligence Community Inspector General. Many of us have subsequently been targeted by this Cabal with threats to our careers, our security clearances, and even our lives. This is not hyperbole, but genuine fact, and this is wrong.

To fix these problems, I propose three principal actions:

- First, Congress and the President should create a single point-of-contact responsible for a whole government approach to the UAP issue. Currently, the White House, CIA, NASA, the Pentagon, Department of Energy, and others play a role, but no one seems to be in charge, leading to unchecked power and corruption.
- Second, we need a national UAP strategy that will promote transparency and help restore the American public's trust at a time when the public's trust is at an all-time low. This strategy should include a whole government approach, including the academic and scientific communities, the private sector, and international partners and allies.
- Third, Congress should create a protected environment so whistleblowers, desperate to do the right thing, can come forward without fear. As it currently stands, these whistleblowers suffer. It is

because of stigma, a code of silence, and concerns about retaliation.

These whistleblowers should be encouraged to come forward in ways that protect them against any forms of retaliation. Policies and procedures should ensure that protection. And for those who refuse to cooperate, it is up to the Members of this Committee and other lawmakers to wield their subpoena power against hostile witnesses and prevent additional Government funding to those UAP efforts that remain hidden from Congressional oversight.

In closing, we as Americans, have never been afraid of a challenge. In fact, we thrive on them. Whether it's eradicating polio or going to the moon. We don't run from a challenge; we take it head on. To the incoming Administration and Congress, I say to you, we need immediate public transparency, and this hearing is an important step on that journey.

If we approach the UAP topic in the same way we as Americans have met other challenges, we can restore our faith in our government institutions. Together, we can usher in a new era of accountable government and scientific discovery. I believe that we as Americans can handle the truth. And I also believe the world deserves the truth. Thank you, esteemed members of Congress, for your time today. It is profoundly appreciated by many.

Three military veterans testified in Congress' highly anticipated hearing on UFOs Wednesday, including a former Air Force intelligence officer who claimed the U.S. government has operated a secret "multi-decade" reverse engineering program of recovered vessels. He also said the U.S. has recovered non-human "biologics" from alleged crash sites.

While the topic of "little green men" did come up, much of the discussion centered on improving processes for reporting unidentified aerial phenomena, or UAPs. The military's term for UFOs (increasingly, UAP refers to "anomalous" rather than "aerial" phenomena, to account for sightings in both air and water). There are also calls to remove the stigma for aviators who report UAP sightings and to ensure oversight of government programs that investigate them.

Retired Maj. David Grusch, who went from being

part of the Pentagon's UAP Task Force, to becoming a whistleblower, told the House Oversight Committee's National Security Subcommittee that he had been denied access to some government UFO programs but that he knows the "exact locations" of UAPs in U.S. possession.

In response to public interest and political pressure, federal and military agencies have shared a trove of information about unexplained aircraft encounters, but Many sightings have been found to be of pedestrian origin, from weather balloons to drones, airborne trash, and birds.

On Wednesday, Defense Department spokeswoman Susan Gough issued a statement saying the Pentagon's inquiries had not turned up "any verifiable information to substantiate claims that any programs regarding the possession or reverse-engineering of extraterrestrial materials have existed in the past or exist currently," as reports The Associated Press.

Grusch also alleged that the U.S. has retrieved "non-human" biological matter from the pilots of the crafts, adding, "That was the assessment of people with direct knowledge on the (UAP) program I talked to, that are currently still on the program." While he refrained from sharing any further information in the public hearing, Grusch offered to disclose details behind closed doors. Grusch said he hasn't personally seen any alien vehicles or alien bodies, and that his opinions are based on the accounts of over 40 witnesses he interviewed over four years in his role with the UAP task force.

"My testimony is based on information I have been given by individuals with a longstanding track record of legitimacy and service to this country many of whom also shared compelling evidence in the form of photography, official documentation, and classified oral testimony," Grusch said, adding that the trove of evidence has been intentionally kept secret from Congress.

Several times during the hearing, Grusch deflected lawmakers' questions, saying he could only elaborate in a SCIF (a sensitive compartmented information facility). Those instances include when he was asked if the government has had any contact with aliens and whether anyone had been murdered to cover up information about "extraterrestrial technology." Grusch said he could not comment.

The former intelligence officer also told the panel that he and several other colleagues have been the targets of "administrative terrorism," and that he has at times feared for his life since coming forward.

"It was very brutal and very unfortunate. Some of the tactics they used to hurt me both professionally and personally," he said, adding that there is currently an open investigation into the matter.

UAP sightings are not rare or isolated

The subcommittee also heard testimony from former Navy fighter pilot Ryan Graves and retired Cmdr. David Fravor about their alleged encounters with aircraft of an unexplained origin. Graves recounted an incident with a flying object off the coast of Virginia Beach in 2014. While flying an F-18, he said, he came upon an aircraft that looked like a "dark gray or black cube inside of a clear sphere." He estimated the size to be 5 to 15 feet in diameter, unlike any aircraft he has ever seen.

Grave claimed the UAP could remain stationary despite hurricane-force winds. He told lawmakers that his squadron submitted a safety report at the time but that he received no official acknowledgment of the incident. According to the former pilot, UAP encounters in that region were "not rare or isolated."

Graves has since founded Americans for Safe Aerospace, a group that supports aviators who have reported UAPs. He stated that the objects that are reportedly being seen by military and commercial pilots "are performing maneuvers that are unexplainable due to our current understanding of our technology and our capabilities as a country." He added: "If everyone could see the sensor and video data I witnessed, our national conversation would change." It is "Incredible technology" unlike anything we have.

Retired Navy Cmdr. David Fravor offered the panel his own eerie account of a UAP encounter that was captured on video in 2004. (The Pentagon released the video to the public in 2020.) Fravor described being flabbergasted when he and three other service members saw a white "Tic Tac" shaped flying object emerge over the San Diego coast in California. "There were no rotors, no rotor wash, or any visible flight control surfaces like wings," he said, as he and the other pilots tried to get closer to the mysterious craft, "it rapidly accelerated and disappeared right in front of our aircraft" leaving no detectable turbulence.

"The technology that we faced was far superior to anything that we had," Fravor said. "I'm not a UFO fanatic. With what we saw with four sets of eyes, we have nothing close to it. It was incredible technology." Fravor said it was several years before any officials followed up on the extraordinary events of the day and even then, he added, "nothing was done."

A 22-year-old from New York City who asked to remain anonymous, "due to stigma that still persists around the subject," told NPR he made plans to attend "knowing that it's something that could be a historic moment."

From an overflow room with about 100 other enthralled spectators, he watched as Grusch, Graves and Fravor, men with long careers in the military, shared their experiences. Out of context, he said, their stories "sound fantastical" but given the credentials of all three witnesses, he said he's a believer. And he wasn't the only one.

"There was definitely a gasp, and everyone was definitely a little bit shocked." He said, "when Grusch was talking about non-human biologics." There was a similar response when Grusch later touched on the personal retaliation he suffered, according to the man.

The hearing is the latest push by Congress to pressure intelligence agencies for more transparency about UAPs, arguing that they're a matter of national security. "UAPs, whatever they may be, may pose a serious threat to our military and our civilian aircraft, and that must be understood," said Democratic Rep. Robert Garcia of California.

"We should encourage more reporting, not less, on UAPs. The more we understand, the safer we will be." Grusch, Graves and Fravor echoed similar sentiments, saying they would like to see a "safe and transparent'" centralized reporting system. The men added that they are hopeful the public discourse is the first step toward eliminating the stigma around reports of UAPs to encourage others to come forward. Graves, the ex-Navy pilot, estimated that only about 5% of UAP sightings are reported to the All Domain Anomaly Resolution Office and the Office of the Director of National Intelligence.

"I urge us to put aside stigma and address the security and safety issue this topic represents," Graves said. "If UAP are foreign drones, it is an urgent national security problem. If it is something else, it is an issue for science. In either case, unidentified objects are a concern for flight safety. The American people deserve to know what is happening in our skies. It is long overdue." Since it was formed last summer, the All-Domain Anomaly Resolution Office has received 366 reports of UAPs.

Transcript: UFOs & National Security with Luis Elizondo, Former Director, Advanced Aerospace Threat Identification Program summarized from Washington Post on June 8, 2021.

Ms. Alemany: [In progress], UFOs or as it's officially identified, officially called, unidentified aerial phenomenon, UAPs. While we're waiting for the unclassified report from Congress on the matter, our guest, Lue Elizondo, the former director for AATIP, the Advanced Aerospace Threat

Identification Program, has some answers. So excited to welcome you today, Lue. Thanks for joining us.

Mr. Elizondo: Jackie, it is my sincere pleasure to be with you today.

Ms. Alemany: So, I want to take us back for a second and set the table for this conversation. How exactly did you get signed in the first place to investigate UFOs for the intelligence community?

MR. Elizondo: Well, Jackie, quite frankly, I was volunteer-told. In essence I had some prerequisite experience that they were looking for. At the time, the organization was new, and they were looking for someone to create a counterintelligence and security portfolio. And I guess because of some of my background running investigations, counterintelligence investigations, and some of my background in technology protection, specifically with aerospace systems, that was a lucrative skillset that they were looking for to create this sub portfolio under AATIP. And that's how I got into the program. I entered the program in 2008. I was asked by its director to come on board and establish this program.

Then in 2010, was when I was asked to take over the effort.

Ms. Alemany: And I'm sure many of you are aware of this. If you are tuning in, you've probably watched the documentary that came out this year, "The Phenomenon." Senator Harry Reid, which this doc outlines, got the program funded. Did you brief him in Congress on these unexplained pilot sightings when you were running the program?

Mr. Elizondo: Jackie, we provide many briefings, mostly through DOD and intelligence community leadership. That information was also provided to times to the staffers and of course our elected officials. It's very important that when you're working in a national security construct that you try to follow the chain of command as much as possible. So, a lot of my briefings were really to more senior level folks in the Department of
Defense and within our intelligence architecture. But there were times, yes, that we were--we would be asked to brief other officials, particularly in the legislative branch and in the executive branch as well.

Ms. Alemany: And right now, everyone in

Washington and really a lot of people around this country are hotly anticipating this unclassified government report on aerial phenomena witnessed by Navy pilots. It's expected to be delivered to the Senate Intelligence community by the director of national intelligence, hopefully by June 25th. The New York Times reported that senior administration officials who were briefed on the findings said that the unusual movements witnessed by pilots did not originate from American military or advanced U.S. government technology, but that's really about the only conclusive finding that has been so far teased from the report. What do you think the likelihood that aerial phenomena are extraterrestrial spacecraft?

Mr. Elizondo: Well, Jackie, that is really the question, isn't it? The bottom line is, up until very recently there were only three possibilities of what this could be. The first possibility is that it is some sort of secret U.S. tech that somehow, we have managed to keep secret even from ourselves for a long period of time. The second option is that it is some sort of foreign adversarial technology that has somehow managed to technology leapfrog ahead of our country despite having a robust and comprehensive intelligence apparatus. And of course, the third option is something quite entirely different. It's a different paradigm completely.

Now as of this week we know through some of the discussions at senior-level leadership that this report has definitively stated once and for all that it's not our technology. And that's hugely important. For 30 years there has always been this undercurrent. These conspiracies say that there was some sort of TR-3B program, a super special technology that has been implemented and we have been very careless about it. I think that argument was finally put to bed this week. So, that leaves two other options. It is a foreign adversarial or it is something quite different. I think we are now beginning to learn, after having heard from the director of national intelligence, I can certainly tell you that we are confident it's not Russian or Chinese technology, and there's several reason for that that.

Ms. Alemany: Yeah, actually, could you go into that. I know you've explained it in previous interviews, but these sightings have happened for the past 70 years, and I know you've said before that you didn't think it was possible for one of our foreign adversaries who have been helpful in providing information on this issue, would be capable of keeping something a secret for so long. Is that accurate?

Mr. Elizondo: That's precisely one of the counterarguments. In fact, if I'm not mistaken, as of today, we had an announcement by former Director of National Intelligence Ratcliffe who said this isn't Russian technology. And as we know during Glasnost and the fall of the Berlin Wall, there was this five-year romance period, if you will, between the United States and Russia where we began really sharing a lot of information. And a lot of their--ironically enough, a lot of their UFO information wound up in our hands, and it turns out that they were experiencing the exact same issues from a UFO or a UAP perspective that we were. So, if you look at really the timelines here, you know, it's looking increasingly less likely that this is some sort of Russian technology.

So, that really leaves China. And some of these reports, you're correct, Jackie, they go back into the early 1950s, and even earlier. And so, what that says is that you have pilots, whether we're describing what we call a white flying tic-tac or a white flying butane tank in the 1950s or a white flying lozenge, if you will--they're all describing the exact same vehicle, craft, if you will, doing exactly the same thing, performing in ways well beyond our current capabilities.

If you look at that from a from a temporal perspective, from a time perspective, it simply doesn't make sense that China back in 1950 would have this beyond next generation technology, mastered it, is able to fly at will anywhere it wants on the face of the planet, and the last 70 years, despite the billions of dollars we've put into our intelligence community infrastructure and architecture, it has--it has managed to evade us.

In fact, China is a country that has stolen quite a bit, spends a lot of time stealing technology from us. And so, one needs to ask the question that if really a country had this technology, would it be necessary to steal, you know, much more basic technology from another country. Furthermore, if you had this type of technology, you probably wouldn't need to invest so much in military because you had this, if you will, checkmate type technology or capability where everything else now becomes obsolete.

So, this goes to your last part of your question. So, do I believe this is, quote, "extraterrestrial"? Let me be very careful before I answer that by saying at the end of the day, Jackie, it doesn't matter what I think or what I believe. What matters is what the data and the facts tell us. From that perspective, it's very important that I had a very simple job, to collect the truth and speak the truth. That's it. Very much as an investigator, which I used to be. We applied the same level of rigor and methodologies we did at hunting terrorists and spies as we did in hunting UFOs.

So, we really didn't care what these were. We were just trying to get to the bottom of what they were. And so therein lies, if you will, a little bit of our approach. We were--we were very agnostic, if you will, or objective about this topic and tried to allow the facts to lead us down a certain path. And that is really what we're doing today. What we're realizing is that the facts are painting a far more compelling picture than what we thought. In this case, you, your audience, they're the jury. So what matters is really what you think about this. And so, the hope here is that the U.S. government can provide the data and the evidence and information and then allow the American people to decide what we think this is about.

You mentioned something very interesting that a lot of people want to talk about and say is this extraterrestrial. I want to delve into where we are with modern day science. We are human beings that people in psychology refer to as cardio-social animals. It means we look at things in extremes because for the first nine months of our existence, we were in our mother's womb. We heard that binary heartbeat of our mother. So, we tend to look at the life in our universe, in that binary way. It is either good or it is bad. It is hot or cold, black or white, up and down. That's how we tend to judge things. Reality in the universe and physics are not binary. They are not binary at all. In fact, there is all sorts of options and opportunities of what this could be.

So, back to your question. Is it from here, or is it

from out there? We don't really know. In fact, there's lots of other options on the table. It could be from--as I've said before, it could be from outer space, inner space, or the space in between. As we begin to learn what quantum physics is and we begin to understand our place here on this little planet, we begin to realize that there's a lot of other options. We judge the universe in five fundamental senses, the ways that we perceive the universe, and that's touch, taste, hear, smell, et cetera. And if you can't--if you can't use those senses to look at something or measure it, then we really can't interact with it. And yet, we know a majority of the universe around us is not perceivable.

There are right now Wi-Fi signals coursing through your body. There's cosmic radiation coming in from the cosmos. There are neutrinos coming in from the sun. There's radar hitting you from the local airport. And yet, these are all realities, and you can't interact with it because we just don't have the tools to do so. Take a beautiful night sky, look at the stars, and you might say, wow, that's really a pretty sky. But if you now take a radio telescope and look at that same spot in the sky, suddenly you begin to see things that you couldn't see before. You see the ultraviolet, you see the infrared spectrum, you see nebula.

So, I guess my longwinded point to all this is that we must keep all options open. If we already know that 99 percent of the universe we cannot perceive or interact with, then there may be other options here. This may not necessarily be something from outer space. In fact, this could be something as natural to our very own planet as us, we're just now at a point we're beginning to technologically be able to interact and collect data. This could be something from under the oceans. This could be something from, yes, from outer space. We really don't know. And this is why I think we really need to take a whole of government approach and look at this, because it is--day by day, it is seeming like more and more this conversation is shifting from a human technology--quite possibly, we don't know for sure yet--but to something far more profound.

Ms. Alemany: But as someone who is more steeped and in the know on the data and the facts, do you have any more narrow idea in that 99 percent of things that we are unaware of what this could be exactly?

Mr. Elizondo: You know, through observations we are--we are quite convinced that we're dealing with a technology that is multigenerational, several generations ahead of what we consider next generation technology, so what we would consider beyond next generation technology. Something that could be anywhere between 50 to 1,000 years ahead of us. And for us, I think it's when you're looking at the observations and these things, how they can outperform frankly anything that we have in our inventory and we're certain anything that our foreign adversaries have in their inventory, then, yes, obviously as human beings we tend to go down that rabbit hole of speculation.

I want to be very careful that I don't offer my opinion in an unqualified manner. I've always stated this is exactly why we need a UAP taskforce. In fact, this is why we need a much bigger, whole of government enduring capability, because at the end of the day we don't know what we're dealing with. Frankly, all options need to be on the table, until they're no longer on the table.

I could offer you my opinion right now, but, Jackie, in all honesty it would probably be a bit of disservice because we frankly don't have enough information yet. We're just now getting to the point as a government, as a society that we are accepting the reality that this is real, whatever it is. I think--I think we need to do a little bit more. So out of respect to you and your journalistic integrity and to your audience, I'm probably going to refrain from offering more of my opinion on that aspect. The one thing I've learned in intelligence is, you can be sure of something and still be wrong. I don't want to mislead anybody.

Ms. Alemany: I'm going to be a little bit of a pest here, and I apologize for my desire for a more black and white answer.

Ms. Alemany: But in common parlance, I guess, is that something that you would refer to as an alien or a time traveler. Is there any sort of way you could, you know, more specifically?

Mr. Elizondo: Sure, so, yeah, I've said before this is something. I guess I may have just said it again, but that this could be something from outer space, inner space, or frankly the space in between. There's a lot of options out there. This could be something perhaps extra hyper dimensional. Now I don't mean extradimensional in a woo-woo sense. I mean, extradimensional in a quantum physics sense. We know that the universe is full of shortcuts and loopholes.

We know, if I may backtrack for just a moment, it took the Renaissance to come to the point where we understand Newtonian physics. We understand what gravity looks like. We still don't quite understand what it is yet, but we understand what it looks like, and we understand force equal mass times acceleration.

So, we had these elegant solutions for our observations of the of the natural world. It took more than 200 hundred years, when comes some cat with crazy hair we called Einstein who now introduces the notion of relativity. It kind of upends real science and turns it 180 degrees and says, well, there is a thing called spacetime, where space and time are connected. They're also stretchable and compressible. And as bizarre as that may be, that is precisely what we're seeing.

So, spacetime can be warped based upon mass or a lot of energy.

Then of course 40 years ago, we really start getting into this other paradigm of science, called quantum physics. Someone described it in this way: a box sits on the ground where a dog walks in, suddenly, two cats walk out. And as crazy as that may seem, that's precisely what we're seeing in these observations with quantum physics, proverbially speaking of course. So, it doesn't make sense, and yet there's this weird duality. Maybe the universe, the speed of light although may be the universal speed limit, there may be some shortcuts and offramps in this understanding of our universe.

So, we are just now scratching the surface of understanding what type of science it may take to do what we are seeing with these vehicles. There is, five specific observables associated with these UAPs (unidentified aerial phenomena). These observables separate them from the rest of anything we would consider terrestrial aircraft or manned aircraft or some type of human-based technology.

Again, I want to be careful not to go too far out on the limb because that's where the speculation starts, and that's also where the danger starts, because we simply don't know yet.

Ms. Alemany: Well, and I guess the other key question here is what do you think the likelihood is that the U.S. government is going to confirm anything?

Mr. Elizondo: Jackie, I think I lost you, but I'm going to go ahead and try to answer the best I can. I think you were asking me what the likelihood is of the U.S. government going ahead and confirming anything in this 180-day report. So let me see if I can go ahead and answer that. Hopefully that was your question because I seem to have lost signal.

So, the 180-day report is, not substantial enough time to do a comprehensive report. In fact, I've told people it takes longer to remodel a household kitchen sometimes than it does to conduct one of these 180-day reports.

Secondly, there's the other issue here that we had COVID and this pandemic that kept a lot of people home for most of that time.

Thirdly, I think if this turns out to be some sort of adversarial technology that has happened to leapfrog ahead of us for the last seven years, Jackie, we're talking about one of the greatest intelligence failures this country has ever seen, probably eclipsing 9/11 by an order of magnitude. It took us nearly three years to come up with a 9/11 Commission report. If this turns out to be some sort of adversarial technology that did happen to technologically leapfrog us, 180 days I don't think is going to be sufficient.

I think what we can expect the report to say is something like this. There are about 100 odd cases out there that are compelling enough that they are displaying some sort of capability, technology that we don't have. Secondly, we don't know what these things are. We have no evidence to suggest that they are from outer space, but at the same time we have no evidence to suggest that they're not. And so, this report will probably be a bit of a placeholder. The one thing we know for sure at this point is that it's not U.S. secret technology. So that takes part of the
30-year argument that this is some sort of secret

Air Force, if you will, weapon platform being tested. That's now off the table. And so now we can focus more, I think, on the foreign adversarial perspective, or hopefully maybe something quite frankly sufficiently different than anything that we had--we had possibly considered before.

Ms. Alemany: And when we're talking about this as a national security threat or as a foreign adversarial threat as you just mentioned, you know, I think we need to talk about China here, which the United States government also views as a national security threat. And China is making big investments to identify extraterrestrial life as a part of their military mission. There's discussion within the community about whether it's better for us to lead the way with confirmation versus China doing so and possibly being dishonest about what they've found a new modern-day space race. Do you think, in your opinion, does it matter which national takes the lead on confirming the presence of extraterrestrial life and who gets to the bottom of this answer first?

Mr. Elizondo: I think you're right, Jackie. They have announced they have established a new

UAP taskforce. This new taskforce is similar. They are using artificial intelligence to do this. We also know there is a playbook by them to try to lead this conversation at the United Nations. It is a multifaceted question you're asking me. There is two parts of me. I'm a little bit schizophrenic about the response. There is the national security side of me that has said always we have these adversaries, these traditional adversaries, and they're going to steal everything they can from us. We should not trust them. Try to cooperate, but don't trust them.

But then there's the other side, which is the non-governmental side of me that tends to be optimistic. Perhaps this is an opportunity for our countries, not to seek disagreement, instead to find common ground. Maybe this may be a new renaissance. Maybe this is an opportunity for our countries to work together on a common good, that involves all of humanity. Maybe like what we did in the Cold War. Where we started working with the Russians toward cooperation. When we started to meet each other in space. I would certainly hope the latter is what happens, but I don't know. You know, that's a great question, because what I hope for may be different than what I expect. And that still needs to be reconciled. So, I don't know if I answered your question appropriately, but that's how I feel.

I would love nothing more than an opportunity to work with our adversaries, our conventional adversaries--Russia, China, let's get everybody to the table. I believe this is a topic that involves all of humanity. I think it affects all of us equally and yet differently, depending on our philosophical, sociological and theological belief systems. So, I guess the kid in me wants this to be an opportunity for us to work together. But I also have a very realistic side, because I've seen what those countries are capable of, and you know, it would have to take a lot of trust for us to do that.

Ms. Alemany: And several of these UFO sightings have been above secret nuclear weapons facilities. Almost every major nuclear power across the globe really has reported and declassified these sightings. You have talked extensively about the connection here, which might be helpful I think for some people to hear in advance of my next question, which is whether the

U.S. government has considered utilizing nuclear-powered naval fleets to lure these kinds of things to further study them.

Mr. Elizondo: Wow. So, Jackie, thank you for asking such a thoughtful question. Obviously, you've done some homework. And I also want to, thank you as a journalist for following this topic, because I know there's a lot of risk involved, and I also know there's been traditionally a lot of stigma and taboo associated with it. So, I want to congratulate you for your courage and thank you and your audience for at least having this conversation.

Secondly, yes, that is--that is one of the concerns we have from a national security perspective, that there does seem to be some sort of congruency or some sort of intersection between these UAP or UFO sightings and our nuclear technology with nuclear propulsion, nuclear power generation, or nuclear weapons systems. Furthermore, those same observations have been seen overseas in other countries. They too have had the same incidents. So that tells us this is a global issue.

Now in this country we've had incidents where

these UAPs have interfered and brought offline our nuclear capabilities. And I think to some they would probably say, well, that's a sign that whatever this is, is something that is peaceful. But in the same context, we also have data suggesting that in other countries these things have interfered with their nuclear technology and turned them on, put them online. So, that is equally, for me, just as concerning. I think that there is certainly at this point enough data to demonstrate there is an interest in our nuclear technology, a potential to even interfere with that nuclear technology.

When you look at all these naval ships out there, let's take the Nimitz battle carrier fleet for example, in some cases you're talking about a nuclear footprint probably bigger than most cities. You have a nuclear-powered carrier with aircraft on board that--and then you have nuclear-powered destroyers. You have nuclear-powered submarines, some of those with nuclear weapons on board, or certainly nuclear capabilities. I'll just say I think it shouldn't be a surprise that maybe there is an increased interest in our capabilities as it relates to our nuclear technology. The Navy is certainly not immune to that.

Mr. Elizondo: Yeah, absolutely. And so, I think there is two congruencies that we see. We see a we see an interest in our nuclear capabilities, and then we have this really bizarre what I don't know if you call it an interest, but there seems to be a connection with water, and these things have a tendency to be seen in and around water, which kind of leads to one of the observables that we've had. There are five distinct observables that set this technology, as I mentioned earlier, aside from everything we have in our inventory.

The first is hypersonic velocity. The ability to change directions instantly. And when I say instantly, I mean human beings can withstand about 9 'g' forces or some of our best aircraft can withstand about 16 'G's. These things are doing 3 to 4, or 600 'Gs' in midflight.

Then there's hypersonic velocity. That is, speeds that are Mach 5 or above, very, very fast. We do have some technology. You mentioned Russian hypersonic and things like that. You know, there are technologies that can go that fast, but then again, you don't expect a hypersonic aircraft to do a 90-degree turn. To put that into context, our SR-71 Blackbird when at 3,200 miles an hour wants to take a right-hand turn, it takes roughly half the state of Ohio to do it. You don't expect it to just kind of do this. And that's precisely what we're seeing. Then the third observable is a bit like cloaking. We call it low observability.

The fourth observable is what we were talking about, and that is trans medium travel and water. The ability for an object to fly not only in our atmosphere, low and high altitudes, but also potentially in a vacuum environment like space and even underwater. Now we do have vehicles that can do that. We have, for example, a seaplane. A seaplane is a plane that can fly, and it can float on the water. But when you look at it, it's neither really a very good aircraft nor a boat because it's a design compromise. And yet what we are seeing are objects that can operate in all these domains or all these environments, seemingly without any type of performance compromise.

So, why are we seeing these things around water is something that we're really kind of scratching our heads with, because we've seen these things.

They've been recorded not only in our atmosphere but there's data to suggest that they've also been tracked by some of our capabilities underwater as well and being able to perform in ways that frankly exceed anything that we know on the planet right now.

Ms. Alemany: And, Lue, unfortunately we only have time for one more question. But I should make it clear to our viewers that you signed an NDA when you were working on this at the Pentagon. Is there any scenario that will cause you to break that NDA if you feel like, for example, this report obfuscates or peddles disinformation about what the findings are here?

Mr. Elizondo: No, ma'am. I will now violate my non-disclosure agreement with the government. I still maintain a security clearance. And the reason is that not because it's my loyalty to the government, because it's my loyalty to the American people. That contract I signed those many years ago was a promise to the American people that I would never violate their trust, period. And I can't violate their trust to gain their trust. It doesn't work that way. So, what I's going to continue to do is doing what

I'm doing now and pushing for this disclosure, pushing for the information that I know to be true because I saw it and so did my colleagues, continue to have this conversation the way I can.

I'll tell you, if it looks like the Pentagon continues to obfuscate, I have made it clear before that there's a possibility I would consider running for some sort of congressional office. I don't want to do that. I'm not a politician. I don't have the political savvy. If I need to put my boots back on to make sure this conversation is had and ultimately allow the American people to have this conversation amongst themselves, then I will do what is necessary short of violating my non-disclosure agreement and violating my trust with the American people.

Ms. Alemany: Well, we hope you'll come to us when you make that decision to run for office. Thank you so much for joining us today, Lue, and thanks for your work on all this.

A long-standing argument about the history of man's origin presented in the Biblical scriptures verses what science presents began with Charles Darwin in his book, The Origin of Species, where he proposes that the primary driving force behind the emergence of man on earth is evolution.

This argument entered the court of law during the Scopes Trial. The Scopes Trial, (July 10–21, 1925, Dayton, Tennessee, U.S.), was a highly publicized trial (known as the "Monkey Trial") of a Dayton, Tennessee, where a high-school teacher, John T. Scopes, was charged with violating state law by teaching Charles Darwin's theory of evolution.

The right for a teacher to teach science in high school, regardless of the controversy from a religious point of view, stems from religion made separate from the elementary school environment just as prayer was also separated from a public-school environment relating to conflicts that might arise between various denominations of religious belief.

Here we will examine some of the found historical records of ancient Sumerian tablets and the indigenous people of ancient India, which define a very different history of human development and origin of man that originate from heaven but certainly not from the biblical narrative.

Apart from the anthropological explanations of early man, yielding to their fears of predators, the occurrence of natural forces such as storms, earthquakes and or volcanic eruptions, it is supposed that a sense of these occurrences provide the basis of imagination of primitive man looking for a calming reaction to attribute all or some of these forces as deity based, such as Ra, the sun God from Egypt, or Zeus, the God of lightning from Greek and Roman culture where the planets enjoyed a revered perspective, such as Mars or Ares, the God of War. Thus engenders the reaction of subservience and awe with such devotion thus attempting to please these deities out of fear of their reprisals.

These primitive reactions of devotion do not explain such devotion arising from more civilized societies that go beyond basic raw exposure to the elements such as fire, storms or the sun and moon. Primitive man would see the moon and the sun as well as some of the planets visible to the naked eye as entities in heaven, perhaps forming the basis for astrological divination.

In the case of the cuneiform writings on clay tablets found at the library of Nineveh in the Mesopotamian plain, some 20,000 tablets having been carved with the unique cuneiform style, once translated define the Sumerian and Akkadian accounts of beings (Gods) coming down to earth in celestial chariots and creating a community called Iridu, in what was referred to as the great Abzu (desert).

These beings of extraterrestrial origin (later referred to as Nibiru, their home planet) were known in the Sumer language as Anunnaki (meaning those from on high came to earth) resided in this region for tens-of-thousands of years, ruling over the indigenous people as Kings.

According to the 'diary' of one of the King's sons, called Ea., later named Enki, described the advanced scientific modifications of indigenous hominids known as Homo-Erectus into Homo-Sapiens, modified for the purpose of creating a mining work force to excavate gold from the earth in that region. The historical account of their existence defined much of the prehistory of the early Sumerian-Akkaden-Babylonian culture. These beings taught agriculture, astronomy, mathematics as well as the skills to speak the language of the visitors and to wield the technology utilized in the mining process.

In the programming of the consciousness of the hominids, an induced quality of devotion to their rulers, reinforcing the concept that their rulers were Gods, and should be worshiped accordingly ensuring loyalty and obedience required to prevent the possibility of an uprising or rebellion.

Likewise, according to the Arian race of beings (recorded in the Bhagavad-Gita and the Rig Vedas (true historical accounts) coming down to earth in celestial carriages or ships called Vimana, were revered as Gods and insisted on their devotion.

The deities of Hinduism have evolved from the Vedic era (2nd millennium BCE) through the medieval era (1st millennium CE), regionally within Nepal, Pakistan, India and I Southeast Asia, and across Hinduism's diverse traditions. The Hindu deity concept varied from personal gods of the Hindu pantheon to major deities in the Vedas, to hundreds of deities mentioned in the Puranas of

Hinduism. The major entities included Vishnu, Lakshmi, Shiva, Parvati, Brahma and Saraswati.

The ancient cultures of Atlantis and Lemuria also had a broad background and long history even before recorded history of the modern era dating back to the 4th millennium BC. Lemuria was part of Gwandana, a quasi-unified continent existing after the singular continent of Pangea broke apart dating back to 3,500,000 years BCE. Lemuria located in the pacific area dates back before 1,000,000 BCE and the Atlantean culture predate 279,000 years in the Atlantic region after Gwandana continued to separate into the known continents of today.

Both cultures have had several encounters with extraterrestrial races such as the Lyrans, Pleiadeans and Draco reptilians from Draconis Major that encouraged a sense of devotion to 'those' on high.

According to Dr. Igor P. Lipovsky, the original homeland of all ancient Semitic peoples, including Hebrews, was not northern Arabia, as is currently believed, but northwestern Mesopotamia. Around 6,000 - 4,000 years B.C., an ecological catastrophe in the Black Sea area forced the Indo-European tribes to migrate outward in all directions. On their way to the south and the south-east, the Indo-Arians displaced and partially mingled with the Hurrians of Eastern Anatolia.

In turn, Arianized Hurrians first displaced the Eastern Semites (Akkadians) from the upper courses of Tigris, and then, at the end of the 3rd millennium B.C., occupied the land of Western Semites (Amorites) in the upper courses of Euphrates. The referencing by the Bible of Harran as the original birthplace of Abraham is the indirect evidence of these ethnic changes. The last wave of Western Semites (Arameans) in 12-11 centuries B.C. was also caused by the movements of Hurrians and Indo-Europeans in northwestern Mesopotamia.

The following account is excerpts from Astral Legends Treatise, relating to NSA-released documents:

Aura Nataru Shari is also known as the Galactic Federation of Worlds (GFW). The Galactic Federation is an organization uniting various sapient species of the galaxy. It was formed a few hundred years before the humanoid expansion of the constellation of Orion, with guiding principles to maintain peace in all galaxies, to serve others, raise consciousness levels, and uphold justice and freedom for all species in every star system.

Most of the GFW are alien humanoids of varying types with diverse skills and abilities, united for peacekeeping, combating the Chi Ahkar Empire. There is an even smaller allied group with the Federation known as the Orion League and the United Worlds Alliance. In December 2020, General Haim Eshed, the 87-year-old former head of Israel's space program, revealed that the United States and Israel have been in contact with extraterrestrial civilizations for several years, and have formed a relationship with the Galactic Federation after once being under the sway of the

Reptilian Empire.

In an interview with Gediot Aharonot, he claimed that this cooperation includes a secret base on Mars, where Americans and extraterrestrial representatives are beginning to collaborate. He also suggested that the American President Donald Trump was discouraged by the Federation from disclosing its existence to the world until the world was ready and introduced appropriately.

The Galactic Federation of Worlds was established following the ratification of the Council Reformation Act over 30 million years ago in the fifth dimension.

Prior to this, there was significant unrest in the galactic community regarding the tyranny of the Chi Ahkar Empire, where colonization, slavery, and genocides were carried out.

After the Orion-Lyran Wars ended, many systems and colonies had developed and declared independence, becoming sovereign nations. However, these new governments were often overlooked by the Council, as the elected representatives primarily focused on their own planet's interests which eventually fell into the hands of the Draco-Chi Ahkar Empire and their alliances. A small, diverse planetary system was inhabited and colonized by the Draco. Eventually, a fierce war broke out among the land's natives. The children of the Nabu and Akari peoples were enslaved.

Amidst this conflict, there was a perilous mission to rescue systems suffering from the slavery and or genocide by the Chi Ahkar. Council members Elessia Aeso and Raul Mourinho initiated a push for a reformation of the galactic governments dissuading them from dealing with the Draco reptilians and their collectives. This movement garnered unexpected support from across the galaxy.

In 2235 CE (in real quantum time), the Reformation began. Over the millennia, elections were held on every planet associated with the Citadel to elect Council members for the new Galactic Council. In early 2240 CE (in real Quantum time), the new Council voted to decide the composition of the Executive Branch, the High Council. As expected, Aeso and Mourinho were among the five elected, along with Udnut Gort of Tujunga, Councilor Tiberion of Vega, and Council member Queen Tiamat of Orion, who replaced Turian Councilor Sparatus.

With the following Reformation, the Federation reorganized trade routes and alliances and began admitting new nations to the Council. The military was also revised. With the ratification of the Galactic Forces Assignment Act, every nation was required to contribute troops to form the Federation military. The organization consisted of several forces, with the bulk of the military composed of humanoid species and insectoid soldiers. By 2250 (in real Quantum time), the Federation had amassed a force equivalent to the alliances of the Chi Ahkar Empire. The Galactic Federation became the main political state of the Milky Way, also known as, Mutter's Spiral. Following the decline of the Earth Empire at the turn of the fourth millennium (in real Quantum time), It was still operating as of the 40th century.

Species whose home worlds are members include Alpha Centaurans, Humans, Ice Warriors, Arcturians, Vegans, Pakars, Pleiadians, Lyrans, and many more from thousands of galaxies. Federation members still enjoy full political authority within their own territories, as the Federation Council is forbidden from directly interfering with internal matters of its member planets. The Galactic Federation of Worlds then united as peacekeepers and holders of justice in this galaxy, and even inter-dimensionally.

The main task for the GFW is to raise awareness among Earthlings about the subversion of their societies by the Chi Ahkar Reptilian Empire, Orion Grey Collective, the Maitre, and Kili Tokerit, helping to identify and expose corrupt institutions and elite manipulation in liaison with these enemies. The GFW now monitors and develops strategies against advanced mind control technologies that the Draco Chi Ahkar Empire is using on Earth.

They monitor extraterrestrial infiltration, work on deprogramming mind control, rescuing abductees, and where possible, remove implants as well as handling many other minor tasks. The main races that are members of the Federation's Council are involved in assisting Earthlings in these efforts. Although the idea of expansion was split among the leaders of the Federation, Mourinho, pushed for rapid growth, and over the next millennia, the

Ashtar Galactic Command, the United Worlds Alliance, the Republic of Lucia in the Orion Star System, the Principal Republic of Asteria in the Vega System, the Republic of Beni, the Feros Union, and over a dozen other planetary governments joined the Federation.

The total number of governments with seats on the Galactic Council had reached 52. The Council of Five was then established as a higher branch of the Federation. The Council of Five is based in the Orion area and was formerly known as the Council of Nine. Created by the Elmenuk from Ardemant and now composed of these five races only. Aurella, Igaroth, Genovo, Raiden, and Emetha, have been involved in protecting Earth long before the creation of the Galactic Federation of Worlds, which they later joined as Council representatives.

They have monitored the earth species since its days as organisms floating in the oceans, by virtue of the north polar satellite, witnessing its evolution into primates, the meddling of the Anunnaki, the various Earth colonizations from all parts of the galaxy, the arrival of evil empires, and the territorial alien wars on Earth. The Council of

Five, currently led by the Igaroth, has met with Earth leaders on many occasions, attempting to influence their decisions with some wisdom, a task that has proven quite difficult.

Unlike the Federation's Prime Directive, the Council of Five changed and does not adhere to a rule of non-intervention. They view intervention as necessary to help incapable worlds avoid fatal mistakes that could lead to destructive paths. The Council met with Earth leaders in 1944 (in Matrix time), and more recently in August 2013 (Matrix time), to discuss the threats posed by the Orion and Chi Ahkar Empires, the Cabal Alliances of Amun-Ra, (also known as Marduk of the Anunnaki), along with the aftermath solutions of non intervention.

The Andromedan Council of the Andromeda galaxy, is akin to a United Nations to our galaxy, also known as the Zenatean Alliance, consisting of 133 representatives from Andromedan planetary systems and races. The Andromedans are the race that taught the Pleiadians their cosmic wisdom and technology. They possess psychic abilities. The Council members are spiritually advanced and

## The Galactic Federation of Worlds

have sent envoys known within spiritual circles on earth as Starseeds to Earth, with a mission to help develop higher Christ consciousness. Operating for thousands of years, they adhere to strict codes and guidelines of conduct. They do not see themselves as saviors, as they believe human souls gain nothing by being saved. This detracts from their own evolutionary experience of finding the progenitors as well as the source within themselves.

The Andromedan-Milky Way governing constellation is located 44 light-years away from Earth and contains 16 main stars with at least 24 confirmed exoplanets, where Andromeda, or M31 galaxy, is a 2.5 million light-years away, within the same line of sight as the constellation, highlighting the significant role of the Andromedan Council in galactic affairs and our solar system They foresaw the future of Earth and recognize earth to be the tipping point in multiverse history. after 5,700,000 years of reptilian occupation.

The first mention of an Andromeda Council originated from Edward Billy Meyer's contact notes in 1975 (in Matrix time). Meyer claimed contact with human-looking extraterrestrials from the planet

Erra in the Taygeta star system of the Pleiades constellation. His claims and evidence were studied by multiple UFO researchers, including Lieutenant Colonel Wendell Stevens, USAF retired, who found them to be genuine. Meyer's contact notes provided insights into the galaxy's history, including human colonies emigrating from one star system to another to escape enemies and planetary disasters (in real Quantum time).

Meyer described how the Pleiadians encountered a highly evolved race of extraterrestrials in the Andromeda constellation, who became advisors to the Pleiadians and their colonies. Besides benevolent groups like the GFW, Council of Five, and the United Worlds, there are also malevolent groups and alliances aligned with the Chi Ahkar Empire for self-service.

The first malevolent group opposing the GFW and the galaxy is the Corporate of Altair, headquartered on the fourth planet of the Alteran system, which maintains dubious ties with the Ashtar and Draconian collectives simultaneously. This diverse group comprises blonde humanoid races, ranging from light melanin to dark melanin complexion with blue or orange hues, and cooperate with a race of greys. The Corporate is not part of the Empire but is heavily involved in abductions and inter-breeding programs. The Ashtar Collective of Sirius B is composed of various humanoid types, including greys, Reptoids, and genetically engineered species known as the Sirian Collective.

Their headquarters is on planet Vorga in the Sirius B system. This group has engaged in conflicts with peaceful Sirians over the ownership of 21-star systems. The Ashtar Collective is also involved with Earth's Shadow Governments and the Amun-Ra Cabal, a group on Earth that operates all secret alliances under the Anunnaki royal named Amun-Ra, or Marduk, ruling Earth under the control of the Chi Ahkar-Drako Empire. The reptilian Draco-Chi Ahkar Empire extends from Cygnus to Perseus and Orion, having colonized over 1000 worlds and establishing a presence on thousands of other planets.

Their symbol is a pyramid with an eye in the middle and a long snake wrapped around in a circle. If the Galactic Federation of Worlds were to cease its operations, significant planet-wide destruction would ensue, plunging Earth into a post-apocalyptic nightmare. The GFW leadership acknowledges that rival extraterrestrial alliances, specifically the Draconian-Reptilian Chi Ahkar Empire and the Orion Alliance Collective, possess greater overall military strength.

However, these rival forces would withdraw from their operations on Earth if the GFW were fully committed to defending it. Previous remote viewing sessions by the MK Ultra group have discussed these opposing extraterrestrial forces, likening them to expat Nazis and Reptilians in Antarctica.

The Galactic Federation of Worlds has bases on Earth in Antarctica, where they share areas with other extraterrestrial beings. They also have underwater bases near the sub-Antarctica base, Northern Sea, Irish Sea and Indian Ocean and Catalina Bay. There are also underwater bases in Atlantic North between Iceland and Ireland, East Pacific, South Pacific North Pole and offshore Alaska.

There are also many Chi Ahkar Empire and alliances bases in between these areas as well. If the Chi Ahkar wins the war, the governments of all dark worlds will utilize a coordinated attempt of the Cabal to deceive the public (through the Time-Loop Matrix) that aliens are coming to invade and destroy Earth. They will use an advanced technology that will fool the public (through combined holographic projections) in believing in going to war and spending trillions for more mass weapons of destruction and genocide.

There are two main reasons for this situation. First, the membership of the Galactic Federation of Worlds is divided. While most members clearly want to help, there are significant doubts within the organization about their actual capabilities, particularly in terms of military strength. Earth is a relatively backwater planet on the periphery of the galaxy, which works in their favor. If opposing galactic forces were to make a major effort to stop the Galactic Federation of Worlds from assisting humanity, it seems clear that those opposing forces could potentially overpower the Federation. However, the calculation is that the opposing forces might not deem Earth worth a major confrontation at this time, especially if it would be costly.

The Draconian Empire and the Orion Alliance have fortunately lost their grasp on Earth in 2021 (in Matrix time), thanks to efforts of the Council of Five and GFW collectives. Many Chi Ahkar minions are in hiding under ground and still control assets on earth and the moon, allowing them to still manipulate humanity's destiny, if humanity does not fight back.

William Bramley describes this process succinctly in his book, The Gods of Evil, which traces centuries of contrived extraterrestrial conflicts orchestrated through controlled political elites to manipulate Earth's evolution. It is the hope that humanity on Earth will rise and defeat this last confrontation to move on to the higher densities of existence (5D).

It is important to remember the Anunnaki royals contributed to the genetic code of altering humans' DNA for worshipping. The Nibiruan Prince Enki gave mankind the ability to turn on or off this at their own behest. You should never worship anyone other than your higher self, and you should always serve the ones you love and others in need.

Remember, the Prime Mover or Source is in you and outside of you. Not God in a religious, or kingly sense, but the All that is everything, the Prime Mover, the source, the creator of all.

Immanuel Velikovski (1895-1979) was a controversial author of several books suggesting a radical interpretation of history and geological upheaval. His best-selling book, *Worlds in Collision* (1950) he argued that the Earth and other planets, had been subject to cosmic catastrophes in historical times.

In his other book, *Ages in Chaos* (1952) writes of parallels he found between biblical and Egyptian history from Exodus to early a Divided Monarchy era, which initiated a debate on the chronologies of ancient history. Then his last work published a posthumously in *Mankind in Amnesia* (1982) he draws on his training as a psychiatrist and psychoanalyst to propose his theory of collective amnesia to explain the inability of people to look at the overwhelming evidence of global catastrophes.

The following is an excerpt taken from Velikovski's book *Earth in Upheaval:*

"The face of the earth, the face of the solar system, the sight of our galaxy and of the universe beyond, all changed from the serene and placid to the embattled and convulsed. The earth is no abode for peaceful evolution for eons uncounted, or counted in billions of years, with mountain building all finished by the Tertiary, with no greater event in millions of years than a fall of a large meteorite, with a prescribed orbit, unchanging calendar, unchanging latitudes, sediment accumulating slowly with the precision of an apothecary scale, with a few riddles unsolved but assured of solution in the very same frame of a solar system, with planets on their permanent orbits with satellites moving with a better-than-clock precision, with tides coming in time, and seasons in their order, a perfect stage for the completion of species; the spider and worm and fish and bird and mammal all evolved solely by means of competition among individuals and between species, from the common ancestor, a unicellular living creature.

"Man was scheduled for a rude awakening from such a blissful and paradisical dream. Whereas not long ago he reproached himself for being a warlike disturber in a peaceful nature. He found himself only imitating aggressive and explosive nature; whereas he relegated the vision of such convulsions into the realm of transcendent and esoteric belief, of Satan and Lucifer and the end of the world, he was awakened to find real indices of the awesome past of his mother earth, ash of extraneous origin covering the ground under her water expanse, a ridge split by a deep canyon encompassing the oceans, bearing evidence of an enormous torque in the embrace of which the earth shuddered, her poles repeatedly reversed, and also wandering; her little sister in this bi-planet system, the moon, no more a lovable luminary to lighten our nights, but a sight of an inferno, a ravished world, with no life left, millions of acres of destruction, battered and molten and bubbled, a picture not new, but not realized in its meaning to earth.

"Our glorious day luminary sends tongues of plasma to lick its planets that splay and harden their magnetic shields to protect themselves from such lovemaking. Radio signals are sent by planets to tell of the anguishes of their inorganic souls, and radio signals come from colliding galaxies, and the placid universe is but an expanse crossed by radiation some of which is lethal, by fragments of disintegrated bodies, by signals of danger sounded from all directions, the only peace coming from the conviction that no great unpleasantness could be in store for us, for the jewel of creation, certainly not by the will of a loving Deity, not by the decree of omniscient science.

"Fair is the outlook considering that this system just emerged from the battles that our ancestors understood as Theomachy, the battle of the Gods, and entered a settled state possibly for a very long period in terms of human lives; fair also is the outlook considering that for almost every peril a panacea was provided…by a protective supreme intelligence? Thus the destructive ultraviolet rays are kept under control by a magnetic shield, and the shield is created by the rotation of the earth and the earth is kept rotating, and though it is not in the center of the universe as man thought only twelve generations ago, it is in the optimal place…at a distance from the sun that assures it of the right measure of heat, so that the water supply in its bulk should stay neither evaporated nor frozen, and the very supplies of water and atmosphere are right for life. In such optimal conditions the living forms that evolved in the paroxysms of nature enjoy another age of growth and plenty…and man, the conqueror of nature which evolved him, reaches for space that always limited him to his native rock and, a victim of amnesia as far as his own recent past is concerned, plays some dangerous games with the atom that he succeeded in cracking open, himself morally not far distant from his ancestor who hit a spark from a flint and made a fire.

His book, Earth in Upheaval is a book about the great tribulations to, which the planet on which we travel was subjected in prehistorical and historical times. The pages of this book are transcripts of the testimony of mute witnesses, the rocks, in the court of celestial traffic. They testify by their own appearance and by the encased contents of dead bodies, fossilized skeletons. Myriads upon myriads of living creatures came to life on this ball of rock suspended in nothing and returned to dust. Many died a natural death, many were killed in wars between races and species, and many were entombed alive during the great paroxysms of nature in which land and sea contested in destruction. Whole tribes of fish that filled the oceans suddenly ceased to exist; of entire species and even generations of land animals not a single survivor was left.

"The earth and water without which we cannot exist suddenly turned into enemies and engulfed the animal kingdom, humans included, and there was no shelter and no refuge. In such cataclysms the land and the sea repeatedly changed places, laying dry the kingdom of the ocean and submerging the kingdoms of the land."

Immanuel Velikovski suffered in humiliation from his critics for his declaration of his truth of his investigations over a ten-year period. As I see it, the greatest disagreement of his theories came to the ultimate confrontation of the classical understanding that catastrophic geological change occurs only over millions of years. Velikovski was advocating that the evidence indicated something much more terrifying, that these changes could occur given the right circumstances perhaps overnight. So, what are these possible circumstances, where these kinds of cataclysms could or would occur?

He was suggesting that the cosmos might be the most obvious source of such a violent turn of nature upon an unsuspecting earth. The most acceptable plausible premise is a meteor strike, what is now referred to as a planet killer; first that its make up would be comprised of a dense material like a metal such as iron and that the size would be at least a mile in diameter; second that the speed of the object would be mile per second offering a velocity that increases its impact when it hits the surface, as well as that velocity and size increase the chances of penetrating the upper atmosphere and not be exhausted by the friction of the air.

The sun is the next candidate for such extinctions, when the sun enters a solar maximum and sun spots are at their greatest intensity where X class flares are generated followed by the ejection of plasma (called a coronal mass ejection) of such magnitude that the energy strikes the earth and disrupts and or destroys electrical equipment, wide-band communications such as HF shortwave radio used by operators would go dark, heat from the flares if they contain high energy waves such as microwaves could start fires that could wipe out cities and the grid of power which we have come to rely on in our modern society.

One such event occurred in 1857, discovered by an amateur astronomer by the name of Kerrington. (Now known as the Kerrington event). In that case, our technology was limited to telegraph, even so, the electrical energy entered the telegraph system and burnt much of the wiring and caused electrical shocks to operators. Today however, our communication systems world-wide is built on a vast network of low altitude satellites and ground-based antennas creating the internet. All the networks and computer systems controlling everything would be lost in a Kerrington event.

The earth still has many active volcanos positioned around the world and some are sitting on great plumes of magma. Some of the volcanoes are large enough to be classified as super volcanos, if they were to erupt it would be catastrophic to the atmosphere and the ash cloud would circle the planet for years causing a change in the temperature causing widespread crop failures contamination of water supplies and bring on a modified ice age.

The kind of catastrophes that smacks of what Velikovski referred to could be due to massive earthquakes at levels of 8.5 to 9 on the Richter scale. These quakes would cause destroy buildings on land as well as Tsunamis (ocean tidal waves ranging in height of 50 -300 meters high (150 ft to 900 ft) causing massive flooding.

There is one other condition that could come from other rogue celestial bodies entering our solar system, of such size like larger than Jupiter having tremendous gravitational pull. If then coming close to earth, could destabilize the earth's rotation or even stop the rotation and make it rotate in the opposite direction, or cause a severe shift in its axis. In any of these cases, the idea of an extinction event Surpasses the asteroid that caused the dinosaurs to go extinct 65, 000,000 years ago.

The Sumerian records tell of an earth crosser, at least 6 times the diameter of earth and has an elliptical orbit of 25,772 years. The perihelion position of it encircling the sun would then be 12,886 years ago, just about the time of the great flood, biblically speaking, it was the flood of Noah. (Gilgemesh in Sumerian records) Everything was destroyed.

One of the geniuses of the 20th century was Nikola Tesla. He created the basis of all our electrical systems making it possible to power the world. Among his greatest inventions along those lines of electricity generation was the AC generator.

He believed that AC or alternating current, was more elegant and offered many advantages over DC. A huge reduction in copper needed was the first benefit which the subway system using the rails lent an easy transmission of power along the ground and could ignore that problem.

The most significant advantage of AC was the use of a transformer, an electrical device designed to convert low voltage electricity to high voltage electricity. This devise used a dual set of magnetic coils each with a different number of windings between the 'primary' or supply side and the 'secondary' coil which delivered the higher voltage to the load or end destination.

Because the electrical energy alternated, the magnetic fields generated between the primary coil and the secondary coil could be magnified by the property of induction (a property discovered by Michael Faraday). Thus, the voltage could be increased substantially and easily by the transformer which did not have any moving parts.

In terms of the distribution of energy, raising the voltage to a very high level, meant that the electrical energy could travel along the outer surface of the transmission line (copper wire) without any loss of power at the point of origin, then the reverse of changing the transformer around so the high voltage applied to the primary could be reduced through the secondary to a lower voltage, and in that conversion, there would be a substantial increase in current without much of a loss of power. Whereas the DC required the full cross-section of the diameter of the copper to carry the same amount of power. So, the wire diameter could be much thinner with less weight and mechanically stringing thin wires over a long distance was more feasible.

All that said, made sense to Tesla, but Edison was a prideful man and very competitive with Tesla. He stood fast in his belief in DC power.

Tesla worked for Thomas Edison for a time and Edison was heavily invested financially in DC electrical power, and his DC system had already powered the subway system in New York successfully. It is still powered by 1200 volts DC on the third rail in that way even today.

The difference between the two is DC stands for direct current and AC stands for alternating current. The problem with DC electrical system was efficient distribution. The difficulty to send large amounts of electrical power over greater distances presented a problem. The amount of copper alone was prohibitive. Curiously, the basis for the competition between these two had to do with something other than efficient distribution.

The New York State prison at Sing Sing was considering the application of capital punishment. The idea was to use a form of electrical energy to electrocute a criminal while sitting in a chair (coined the electric chair). This test between AC and DC would determine who would get the contract for the design of power distribution at Niagara Falls. The prison tried both ways and DC power just exploded the body of the criminal with little or no pain involved because death was instantaneous. When AC was applied, the time involved was much longer and indicated greater suffering on the part of the criminal subject. Tesla's AC was chosen, and he won the Niagara contract. Edison and Tesla had a falling out at that point.

His designs for the AC generator were equally brilliant and did not require the use of conducting brushes to initiate rotation of the motor, as the brushes suffered significant losses at the contact points and the carbon brushes would wear out easily.

Tesla was not enthralled by the need to string unsightly wires to transmit energy across greater distances. He began to explore the development of higher voltages.

He was aware of other properties within the electrical phenomenon, such as the property of resonance. (a property that defines a sympathetic relationship between two objects and the energy fields between them.) He became inspired when he studied the phenomenon of lightning and the relationship between the discharge of that enormous power occurring between the ionosphere and the earth.

He invented a special transformer for the purpose to recreate lightening. (the famous Tesla transformer) was the result. He wanted to get away from the need to use wires to make a connection or return path of electrical energy. The electrical energy at very high frequencies became more like electromagnetic waves or a form of radio waves than compared to electrical energy traveling through wires.

At the New York World's fair of 1939, he demonstrated his lightening devices and presented evidence that high frequency was not lethal. He amazed his spectators by allowing the lightening to travel over his body and shoot outward from his fingertips to large copper spheres. More importantly, he also demonstrated motors running on only one wire using his radio transmission techniques. Some of his concepts in this regard is still a mystery today. Now anyone can build a tesla transformer, however his design required a third coil, which no one to this day understands why.

He was convinced that wireless transmission of electrical power was not only feasible but held the promise of free electrical power to everyone on the planet.

To prove his theory, he set up a lab for this purpose in Colorado Springs, Colorado. He believed that he could create resonance with the frequency of the earth's ionosphere by building a tower powered by his special transformer. He believed that the earth was drawing unlimited power to rotate the planet directly from the sun. That power was transmitted via lightning bolts to the earth from the ionosphere. So, he planted into the ground several hundred specially constructed light bulbs spread across a field at some distance from his laboratory and his transmission antenna.

After his transformer achieved resonance, the light bulbs illuminated without any connection other than the earth, However the backlash of the transformer caused a blackout at the local power station which caused quite a stir among the locals! He didn't care about that, but his experiment was a success and then he began to design the ultimate a Full-sized tower later at War cliff, New York.

His dream collapsed when his primary financial source (J P Mprgan) withdrew support, when he told the truth to Morgan of the purpose of his invention. Morgan wanted nothing to do with a project that would remove the immense business opportunities and financial rewards of charging for electrical power usage. I had the privilege of having access to his personal notes from his Colorado experiments provided by the Yugoslav archive Library. In those notes he stated that to understand the secrets to the universe, three elements were key: frequency, resonance and vibration.

Here then, I will attempt to explain how those ideas apply to the laws of alchemy as it relates to human evolution. By evolution I mean the raising of the vibration of the human body and mind through frequency, resonance and vibration, otherwise described as ascension. Alchemical principles can be understood and applied by way of two paths: physical alchemy and spiritual alchemy.

The goal of alchemy is the transmutation of base elements into precious elements. On a physical level, this is achieved through the proper application and combination of pure elements and geometry. A perfect example of this is in the creation of nuclear fission. The first atomic pile (Chicago Pile 1) was built and tested beneath the stands of Stagg Field at the university of Chicago, Illinois on December 2, 1942, which marked the first controlled nuclear chain reaction achieved by humans. The shape (geometry) of the pile was a small pyramid, with pure uranium and pure carbon (pure elements) the secret to its success was through applied resonance.

Spiritual alchemy is achieved in a similar fashion only here we are using the human body as the base element. The human body has some elements which form together a homeostatic energetic system. Each human body is unique by virtue of its resonant frequency in total. The contributing energy that defines that resonance relates to the sympathetic relationship to the earth's energy components, (between the earth and the ionosphere and the sun) and the emotional and mental consciousness of the individual.

There is a plethora of older writings stemming mostly from the middle-ages, that define the alchemical process by personal experimentation, mostly from one called Paracelsus, and curiously, another less well known for his alchemical experiments was Sir Isaac Newton. Perhaps hundreds of other brave individuals in the past, believed in and practiced the art of alchemy. One of the elements used in this practice was Mercury. Unfortunately, many met their demise when improperly cooking this metal because the vapors

## Ascension, Not Staying the Same

were toxic, and most cases resulted in insanity or death. As an aside, Mercury was also used in the manufacture hats at the turn of the century. They also suffered in a similar way, as the saying goes; "mad as a hatter".

In the author's opinion, these aspirants of the spiritual prize of the "philosophers stone", the element that is described as the result of physical alchemy, provides to the experimenter eternal life, perfect health, and unlimited wealth were misguided and misunderstood the ancient writings such as Thoth's Emerald Tablets. Thoth purported to be an Atlantean scientist having escaped the deluge of the empire and entered Egypt to influence the indigenous tribes with his esoteric science.

With the basic understanding that all physical substance vibrates at specific frequencies based upon mass and geometry. Then also there needs to be the understanding that the basic elements: earth, fire, water, air and spirit all vibrate at their base frequency. With the alchemical application of geometry and resonance, each element can be transformed, meaning their frequency can be changed, meaning elevated.

Here, I will use the metaphor of the classic blacksmith working his skill and art with metals. His goal is the transformation of the metal which is hard and not malleable. His goal is to change its physical properties from hardness to softness allowing him to alter its shape into a shape he desires, whether it is a sword, a plowshare, or a horseshoe. First, he possesses an iron caldron with several combustibles, such as coal, needed to establish the conversion of the coal into the element of fire, the first phase of the process. Besides the obvious tools of his trade, that is, an anvil, and a hammer. He must also possess a bellows and a quenching agent, then comes the use of the troth of water. The bellows is key to the second phase of the transformation.

The proper use of the bellows requires the knowledge of how to alter the frequency of the third element, air. As is the case of the other elements, air has a standing frequency (vibration of molecules) at sea level. (as a point of interest, in Atlantis, the engineers knew that all elements have many different frequencies such; 52 kinds of fire; 52 kinds of water; 52 kinds of air; and 52 kinds of earth, and 52 kinds of spirit)…note: the Tarot deck

## Ascension, Not Staying the Same 223

has 72 cards. 20 are the court cards…the fifth suit called the Major Arcana, and 52 cards are the Minor Arcana which are a suit of hearts(cups), a suit of spades (swords), a suit of clubs (wands), and a suit of diamonds (pentacles). I mention this because the truth-sayer, or oracle is an alchemy-based tool, the truth becomes the finer element arising from the geometry of the lower elements or cards.

The bellows is a large canvas bag, a 4-sided flap open at one that defines a large cavity. Each side of the larger faces of the bag can be closed together looking much like a collapsed umbrella. This shape constitutes the geometry needed for the transformation of air. At the other end, the bag tapers down to a small round orifice to allow the air to pass through.

When the bellows is open, the cavity captures some air from the nearby area. When it is quickly closed, the air is squeezed toward the small opening. This action speeds up the air while it is under pressure. The effect of the pressure increases the frequency of the air molecules and then rushes toward the orifice. As the air is forced to pass through the small opening it increases its frequency even more.

The standing vibration of fire from burning coals is red in frequency. The blacksmith needs to raise the vibration of the fire from red to the blue frequency(a hotter fire). Now the blacksmith places the metal into the burning coals and aims the bellows toward the fire. The action of a frequency mixing principle called heterodyning, the faster frequency of air mixes with the red frequency and makes it turn blue. This is repeated until the metal becomes red hot.

Some hammering begins. Time is important with alchemy. One who is practicing Alchemy must be aware of slowing the transformation down(this is where the quenching with water begins).

In the body, the way of working with the air is important. Several elements must be stimulated throughout the body. Every cell of the body has a core of energy(this core is called the mitochondria). Normally these are at a static state and vibrating uniquely by each organ, unless called upon through movement. Three states are required for the final phase of transformation to occur. First, a chain reaction must be created. Then a stage of

## Ascension, Not Staying the Same

avalanche must occur. Then a singularity must arise (this where all mitochondria are synchronized and at the same frequency.)

When the mitochondria are brought into stimulation, increased vibration occurs as an excess of oxygen is brought into the lungs where the blood circulates and brings the oxygen (magnetic force) into each cell. Note: the breath must not be abdominal. It must be uniquely upper thoracic. The breathing should be long breaths connected with each inhalation and each exhalation. (this is called bellows breathing). The sensation will begin at the extremities (feet and hands as a sense of tingling) this is done until the entire body is buzzing and tingling, which is normal for this practice. This process is called a chain reaction. It is slow at first but begins to accelerate, this is called an avalanche.

Now the mental focus is brought into play. Bringing the mental focus upon the lower abdomen while exhaling completely as force of pressure pushes down and back toward the spine is applied to move the vacuum down into the sacrum holding it there for as long as is possible. As the inhale cycle begins, the attention is slowly brought up the spine drawing the vacuum (negative attractive force) which brings the consolidated mitochondrial energy into the hippo campus. Rest the attention onto the pineal and pituitary while continuing to press and squeeze the crystalline fibers of the pineal until the glands respond by releasing their vital fluids. As the fluids join at and cross the Claustrum there comes the singularity where the eye becomes one. Repeat this process until there is fixed that consciousness into an expanded state. Then the awareness of the quantum is aroused joins the singular awareness of self and then comes enlightenment and full awakening.

Now it's time to talk about the nature of the prison on planet Earth. In the last decade there has been extensive mathematical analysis by several scientists to develop more sophisticated virtual (meaning creative) as well as augmented reality (meaning actual or real world external) displays. Military applications of this technology are used for pilot 'heads-up' displays superimposed on the face plates of their helmets or projected upon the aircraft canopies to offer technical data to the pilot without turning away their attention from circumstances outside the aircraft.

Game developers use this math to create algo-rhythms to develop simulations for warfare training programs while other game developers wish to create more realistic and full emersion techniques for entertainment purposes.

Augmented (real) reality simulation uses real world calculations for comparison. In their analysis of real-world parameters, the scientists began to realize that real world calculations use the exact same formulas as virtual world calculations. The only difference is the sophistication level, meaning how detailed their virtual presentations can be depends on the higher math required.

Philosophically, this discovery brought about a suspicion. The 'real' world reality might suggest our perception of the real world might be a projection upon our senses, instead of the real physical reality we have come to accept as true existence. Our acceptance of our surroundings then supplanted by an advanced race of alien intelligence wishing to snare our perceptions and hide the actual real world around us. This startling idea began to take hold and now that disturbing suspicion is running rampant among the scientific community.

Neil Tyson Grayson, a popular physicist celebrity enjoys discussing scientific ideas to the public and has suggested that perhaps we may live in an alternate reality inside of an alien projected reality designed to hide from us the true nature of our surroundings. At first, he could not accept this supposition, but he has accepted this possibility within fifty percent of probability. Considering this idea as factual brings up the obvious question. If so, then what are the alien intelligences hiding from our perceptions?

The spiritual guide to the author has revealed the answer to this question and, that answer is not one you would not like to hear and understandably so. That idea is presented here for your review and consideration. It is an awful conclusion, should you consider it as fact and not as fantasy or pure science fiction.

The CIA and NSA agencies would choose to control the narrative here to explain away some of the truth about our world. Thus hide their agendas with alien intelligence and their secret military industrial complex receiving technological help from certain species that live here under ground and under water bases secretly.

They would hide the secret pact with these alien species in 1952 to reveal their exchange for the alien technical help at the expense of millions of people selected for hybrid alien-human experimentation through an unlawful abduction program. The government agenda to allow the probing of our species is hidden in plain sight by the spreading of misinformation and defining the truth as conspiracy theory about the existence of alien life existing beyond our planet. Further, that evidence is strong in historical artifacts that they have been visiting the planet for thousands of years up to the present, and the government is guilty of a coverup since the first recent crash of a UFO in Roswell, New Mexico in 1947.

They not only have collected the remains of many UFOs, but alien biological entities as well. Further, the secret space program has alien life forms working within the space program alongside humans, a discovery made by a computer hacker, Gary Mckinnon, who hacked into the Pentagon database and noted alien personnel listed on a military industrial complex roster. He now lives outside the US because there is an outstanding warrant for his arrest for espionage and is labeled a traitor.

After World War II, during 'Operation Paperclip', more than 1100 Nazi scientists were brought to the United States cleared of all war crimes and allowed to assist in America's space program. The leading rocket scientist was Werner Von Braun, designer of the Jupiter C Rocket used to put American astronauts on the moon in 1969. Von Braun admitted to the press once when asked how the Germans were able to advance their technology so fast during the war. He pointed to the sky and declared, "from our friends out there". The is the lesser-known fact that the major portion of the original NASA personnel were consisting of Nazis. This shows that our American government is willing to set aside their moral scruples for the chance to gain the advantage and superiority of military power over our proposed future enemies and to advance their secret agendas.

Perhaps there are already humans living on the moon, an artificial satellite, and on Mars alongside aliens in their military facilities. It's the author's belief that humans have been a space faring race for hundreds of years. According to the secrets behind the veil, the matrix of illusion, hiding the awful truth that Earth was destroyed more than 800 hundred years ago. That mankind escaped the destruction by the colonization of the solar system and beyond. So, if earth is gone then what is this simulation for? Let us descend, down the rabbit hole a bit further.

So, if the earth was destroyed long ago, then why is it still here? The answer to that would suggest that this so-called reality of life on earth is a past projection, a 'virtual time loop' before the destruction occurred, recreated by an alien race to provide a human farm that supplies food in the form of strong human emotions and meat, yes, that's right. You heard it correct! The movie, 'The Matrix' was not all that wrong. Only different in some of the details. I have already explained the origins of humanity 450,000 years ago and their manipulation of our genetic sequence for their own needs. Then they left the planet. They were the gods 'that from heaven to earth came' the translation of Sumer language as the Anunnaki.

The truth is that many alien species have come to earth over the real past. The Anunnaki were not only ones. After they left another more brutal, Draconian species arrived and took over the gold mining operations from the Anunnaki. They also planned to make Earth their own and humans as their slaves. Like the Anunnaki, they were reptilian, but a different variant of the species.

They came from the Mica star system. They were known as the Arcturians, and renowned for their military might in the galaxy, even until today. The alien biological entities warned the American military that the Draconian species will return. Humans need to be ready! The Draconian warriors established a base here, then there began a rebellion in their home world system and most of the garrison left to settle the rebellion and promised to return. They left a contingent here to continue the mining operations. But after several thousand years passed, the contingent decided they were never coming back. The remaining Draconian warriors decided to claim the Earth for themselves and keep the gold to barter later.

Light in the home world system was dim and compared to our sun, the light was painful which made surface dwelling difficult. So, they built vast domiciles below ground which, over time spread to many areas around the earth. They longed to live on the surface of the planet, as they had done in their home world. Over many thousands of years, they began to abduct humans and experiment in their laboratories to create a hybrid of their species that could eventually move to the surface.

They saw the calamity approaching the earth and used their time travel technology to reverse time in the near region of the solar system creating an endless loop that would ensure their existence and provide a continuous source of food from the human stock. To prevent the livestock from discovering the truth of their enslavement while maintaining control, they built a matrix of reality, a zoo of sorts, suitable to keep the livestock healthy. Then they realized there needed to be a way of managing the growth rate of the livestock while at the same time providing a source of negative emotional energy which, was an exotic kind of drug they came to crave. Using their powerful mind control technique, they would instill in the humans an increase in their base instincts of survival to increase their aggression. War was added to the emotional mix based on the need to dominate through territorial conflict. Realizing that death could be a way of escaping the prison, they usurped and hacked the reincarnation process to keep humans from leaving the earth to return over and over unconsciously, keeping the livestock plentiful through recycling. There you have it. It's not pretty, but like it or not, we are prisoners on a slave planet.

The approximate date of the flood is said to be around Noah's time, occurring around 12,500 BCE. This time also corresponds roughly to one half the orbit of the binary twin (the dwarf star) to the main sequence star Sol. According to Sumerian records, Nibiru is one of 6 planets orbiting the dwarf star. Also, according to Sumerian accounts, the Anunnaki time of a Shar is 25,772 years of earth time. The complete orbital path would be for the dwarf star to complete its path through the aphelion(nearest) and perihelion (farthest) of its elliptical orbit around our sun.

Astronomers estimate that the orbit of Neptune has a span of 39.5 AU (3.7 billion miles) from the sun. The AU (astronomical unit) represents the distance the earth is from the sun (93,000,000 miles). The dwarf star sits at the outer edge of the Kuyper belt which is about 30.7 billion miles (which is approximately 327 AU from the sun).

According to the simplified (non-calculus) formula for the calculation of the circumference of an ellipse is: $C = 6.28$ times the square root of $A2 + B2 /2 + 3.14(A+B)/2$, which provides an approximate distance and time of the ellipse at

25,772 years.(the same period of the precession of the equinoxes) a measure used to gauge recorded events through the 12 houses of the zodiac or (2,147 years each).

So, the Anunnaki would say that the orbit of Nibiru, their home world, would take one shar to complete. The average life span of the Anunnaki rulers from Nibiru according to the Sumerian King's list was between 2 and 3 shars, (approximately 51,544 -77,316 earth years), based upon their orbital period. Just as our orbital time for a human life span is based upon the orbital period of earth around the sun, a one year/orbit providing the 70–100-year life span.

Biological laboratory evidence of unimpeded development of human tissue is approximately projected to be 1000 years. This corresponds roughly to biblical accounts that reflect the preflood human life span at the time of Enoch (365 years), Noah (950 years) and Methuselah (969 years). According to the Anunnaki ruler Enki's personal record, those hybrid Anunnaki-Adamite offspring born of the earth in later generations did not live as long as their Nibirian counterparts, then closer to the 175-year life span. This would suggest that the sidereal orbits about different solar system suns may control the genetic program of lifespans of organic life upon the planets of those different solar systems.

According to the collision event which occurred with Tiamat 3.5 billion years BCE, 3 billion years BCE later the earth was formed. Then another 500 million years of evolution that developed several hominids like the Homo-Erectus, which after the Anunnaki arrived 450,000 BCE, genetically modified these hominids into Homo-Sapiens (The Adamu or Adamites). According to the Sumerian creation account, (the 'Enuma Elish'), and the Sumerian flood account, ('the Epic of Gilgemesh') which relates perhaps to the Persian Gulf flood, King Anu ordered the extinction event upon the earth at the next orbital cycle of Nibiru passing nearest to Jupiter and upon a close pass to the earth caused the earth to wobble more than 40 degrees. This caused the tectonic plates (continents) to slide around and generate 2000 ft tidal waves over all continents. This is the same flood account offered in the Hebrew flood narrative of Noah, which is estimated between 10,000- and 12,500-years BCE.

So, Gilgemesh is the Sumerian survivor counterpart of the Hebrew flood narrative and survivor Noah.

There are two modern geological theories vying for the top theoretical narrative to explain these geological calamities. First, that non catastrophic geological changes of this magnitude could only occur over millions of years. Second, that sudden catastrophic geological changes could occur from sudden chaotic forces that shift the earth abruptly. Perhaps when the earth's magnetic field collapses to reverse polarity. As the earth's core stops spinning and the field flips, this could trigger tectonic plate(s) to move around which could occur almost instantly.

The magnetic field collapse would also expose the surface to extremely low temperatures. Any unsuspecting animals standing near a low atmospheric pressure (a magnetic hole stretching out into space) would surely become quick frozen before they knew what was happening. The proof of this is from mastodons found frozen solid with fresh flowers still undigested in their mouths, which could only mean that the freezing process had to occur in a matter of minutes to perhaps hours. The idea that this could only occur in millions of years does not match easily to the critical analysis of quick freezing of animals .

Despite any controversy around biblical authority and relevance, there is a reference in some of the verses in the book of Mathew of the New Testament, relating to a question put to Jeshua (Jesus) regarding the end time. Taken to mean when the world ends, and when and how would they know the coming of it.

A precise interpretation of these words would relate to the 'end of the system of things', not the end of the world. Unfortunately, the incorrect view is sort of implied by religious scholars. The author believes that this is due to the interpretation that the kingdom promised will be after the earth passes. This indicates the separation of earth from heaven, which is where the kingdom of God resides. This gives rise to the idea of letting go of the old earth of the third density. The new earth of the fifth density (new frequency) becomes part of the 'new kingdom.'

Then in another passage it is said, "those who are meek of spirit will inherit the earth," meaning the old earth of the third density frequency. Perhaps suggesting those who are weak of spirit are not developed enough to enter the kingdom of heaven, meaning not being able to shift to a higher frequency of consciousness. Even though theologians must conclude those that are left behind in the old earth (third density) are simply not ready to make the shift not because of God's punishment. Simply put, those of 'meek or weak spirit' are allowed to continue in their own time to develop, who are not high enough in frequency yet to merge with the new kingdom of the fifth density.

So, the end of the system of things refers to the socio-economic, spiritual and political system which governs and runs all lives. All that will come to an end. That would yield a time of the new kingdom. (a different density or dimension) to become the new existence including a new earth and sun. The process of that transformation is occurring right now coming directly from the sequence star Sol, through its multiple flares and coronal mass ejections slamming into all the planets encouraging the shift in frequency to the fifth density.

The earth is near the end of its precession, meaning the twin system appears in our system and may be a tumultuous impact in its effect. Which may mean a shift in density from the third density to the fifth density at this time.

The prison that binds us will be broken. We, the slaves of the intruders, will be set free, free to feel and have our own thoughts, desires and aspirations without any concern for outside forces to interfere or seek to control and manipulate us for their own sake. There would be no more wars because that influence would also be gone in the new density.

The author would say that most people view the earth as a round ball. In truth, it is more ablated in shape, meaning it bulges at the equator more than at the poles. This is because the earth spins on an imaginary axis that runs through the planet pole to pole. It is the centrifugal force effect that pulls at the center of the planet all round its girth and draws it outward. The distance it has grown at the periphery is related to the speed of rotation. Were the earth to rotate faster it may break up due to the centrifugal effect, meaning the centrifugal forces can be larger than the combined effect of the nuclear forces binding matter together including the addition of the gravitational force.

The concept of tectonic plate movement is an accepted truth now. To be clear, these tectonic plates correspond to the continents spread across the globe. With the earth's crust only being about 40 miles thick, it sits on a lower layer that is fluidlike which moves slowly (highly viscous), the plates are free to move about until they crash into other plates. In that case, mountains are created from the crust buckling upward.

Speaking of centrifugal forces, the south pole which includes the Antarctic continent, does not sit centered on the earth's polar axis, it is a bit off. The polar ice cap sits on top of the entire continent. The ice is more than a mile thick in most places with even deeper thickness in other places. That ice has formed quickly, before the earth could absorb it. So, the glaciation sets on top of the continent adding to an imbalance of mass circling the axis pole. The additional mass will cause the earth to become unstable and wobble, which is about 40 miles from the center.

The centrifugal force at the equator counteracts the force at the poles due to the imbalance of the weight of the ice pack. A certain balance of forces keeps the wobble at its present condition. It is a delicate balance and could be disrupted easily, where an outside force could disturb that balance. On the other hand, the ice sheet covering Antarctica is ever growing so, the balance of forces could be interrupted causing a calamity of major proportions. This 'internal' event could take thousands of years for the ice sheet to overcome the balance of both forces. This may be the case at certain junctures during the equinox period. Glaciation forming at the poles is then cyclical.

Earth changes can occur abruptly at any time. The earth passes through some very complicated spaces filled with many obstacles of ice and rock and are of many sizes (comets and asteroids) that freely move around like a pinball gallery and planets with their moons add to the complexity of the picture. The earth wobbles through the Equinox, a period of 25,772 years. On the second side of that orbital period of 12,886 years, the solar system goes through a collision burdened space possibility when it engages with the Perseid asteroid zone, or the twin star of our system, the other solar system that lies near the Kuyper belt.

A lot of geological evidence points to a cyclical period of chaos when the conditions on the earth are altered drastically. The writings of Immanuel Velikovsky discusses this in his work, Worlds in Collision, the kind of forces such as, impacts or collisions that have caused some of the extinction events in the past.

Velikovsky's ideas were met with great controversy from mainstream astrophysics. Charles Hapgood, wrote about the crust moving around in his work, Earth's Shifting Crust, describing the actual conditions of the earth's crust and the dynamics involved with the liquid mantel below the crust that helps to provide a fluidity to the crust movement which follows the polar and equatorial centrifugal force dynamics at work.

Many astrophysicists believe we are near the end of an equinox cycle. Using the flood evidence as a benchmark, approximately (12,886 BCE) suggests how to begin the process of determining where the earth is along the Equinox path.

## Tribulation. Precursor to Ascension

We can start with the full orbit of the equinox, which is 25,772 years. Then half of that period is 12,886 years. If we assume that the record of the last flood corresponds to the time when the two solar systems were colliding, perhaps then, there is another 265 years left until the solar system will begin to engage with the sister solar system. This may refer to the biblical time also called 'the end of days.'

The good news is, since the sister solar system is 30-degrees at an angle to the plane of the ecliptic (imagine all the planets revolving around the sun on a flat surface.) Now imagine all the planets and moons revolving around the dwarf star coming in at a 30-degree angle to the flat surface (plane of the ecliptic) of our planets. The chances of a collision are much smaller than if the sister solar system were also on the same plane of the ecliptic, disaster would be guaranteed with many collisions. Also, astrophysicists have determined that galaxies also collide such as the Milky Way and Andromeda are colliding even now but very slowly. This process will take many millions of years to complete. So, we can breathe easier and remove that concern from our immediate timetable.

The timing of the individual orbits of our solar system planets and the dwarf system planets would need to be precisely timed, so that there is no conflict. Prehistorically speaking, there must have been countless times when the two solar systems merged within each other, during a complete precession period without incident. Given that this idea is true, then a resonant circulatory harmony arises between the two solar systems inherently aligned because of their vibration energetically. The two stars are twins, so it may be the suns of each system control the movements of the satellite planets revolving around them, meaning their speed and orbital distances. Once the systems stabilize, collisions would not happen ordinarily.

That said, it must be concluded that the flood event must have been caused by another force that imbalanced the orbital frequencies. This allows for a collision from a temporary instability such as, a severe wobble of the planet setting in motion the crustal shifting.

This concept then corresponds to the Sumerian accounts of the Anunnaki King Anu, who declared that he wanted to cause the extinction of the Nephilim and the Adamites from earth which they had created. So, King Anu shifted the gravitational forces to influence the course of Nibiru's orbit closer to Jupiter causing the speed of Nibiru to increase (the sling shot effect). Then, when Nibiru passed the earth quickly, it caused the earth to slow down abruptly creating a disturbance of the centrifugal forces and the plates to shift suddenly resulting in the massive global flooding.

The common belief in the non-catastrophic geological theory defines the last glacial period to be 120,000 - 11,000 years ago. The author believes that it is more likely that due to the earth core slowing down and the magnetic field collapsing exposed the earth to the extreme cold of outer space in certain regions near the new poles, established in the upheaval process. It is suspected that 'Antarctica' was originally a lush and semi-tropical continent called Atlantis before the flood and sat at or near the equator. After the pole shift, Atlantis submerged below the flood waters and began to slide to the new pole area where glaciation formed over the continent as it is today.

Now we call it Antarctica.

Ancient maps of the Antarctic continent accurately define land below the ice pack. Those maps, such as the famous Piri Reis map compiled by the Ottoman admiral and cartographer in 1513, related the idea that his map was taken from even older maps which are now lost to antiquity. So, glaciation can occur very quickly, meaning the ice age occurred immediately following the flood.

In these modern times, there is some talk amongst religious circles and some fringe spiritual reports that a time will come when there will be three days of darkness upon the earth.

The author's first reaction to this news, was dubious. Regarding this kind of prophetic information stemming from scriptural references, leads to many misinterpretations and are rampant these days. Yet, I began to think about the Dwarf system of planets sliding through our solar system and then suddenly, I remembered the description of the Anunnaki home world Nibiru. It is huge and the astrophysicist's estimation from Nibiru's movement has a dramatic impact upon the orbital stability and wobble about the two outer planets nearest the

Kuyper belt, Neptune and Uranus of our solar system. The theory of planet X survives much controversy regarding its existence because we have not seen any evidence of it.

The mathematics define the probability of an additional outer planet. That mathematical prediction also suggests the location and probable size relating to the strange behavior of the outer planets which would respond to the presence of a planet that voluminous, carrying a heavy magnetic and gravitational field stands defiant against those who would scoff at this theory.

Now with the James Webb telescope there is hope that it will be seen soon. The size of planet X would correspond to perhaps 6 -10 times the size of the earth. That said then, were it to enter our solar system and come between the earth and the sun, it could easily block out the sun for three days because of its slower transition as compared to when the moon comes between the earth and the sun. There is a darkening in some areas on the earth where a full eclipse in underway. The moon is smaller than earth but its distance away from the earth almost covers the sun during the eclipse except for an outer rim. In the case of Nibiru, it would completely blackout the sun and because of its slow transit time, may take three days.

## Crop Circles, Alien Messages

A crop circle, or crop formation, or a corn circle is a pattern created by flattening a crop, usually a cereal grain. The term was first used in the early 1980s. Crop circles have been described as falling within the range of hoaxes as described by Taner Edis, professor of physics at Truman State University.

Usually noted by obscure natural causes or sometimes attributed to alien origin or caused by some supernatural source which is often, suggested by fringe theorists. Officially, these claims have no scientific evidence for such explanations and that the official statement is consistent with human causation.

As with UFO phenomenon, the official explanation is too obvious of a negative conclusion especially when one begins to examine the evidence of a particular kind of circle. Many years ago, the author was scouting the location for a potential excursion with a group of like-minded individuals interested in mystical and or unusual artifacts that emerge historically and otherwise mythically in history in other countries. England was designated for a potential destination for one of my excursions because I was interested in the Arthurian legends of King Arthur, Sir Lancelot, Queen Guinevere and the purported locations of their famous habitat called Camelot.

While scouting the areas of Stone Hinge, the Avebury complex of standing stones, and the Tor of Glastonbury, I had the privilege of witnessing such an occurrence. In contrast to those crop circles or crop formations, archeological remains can cause cropmarks in the fields in the shapes of squares and circles, but these do not appear overnight and are always in the same places every year. One point during the review of interesting locations was Bath, England. This was the location of an ancient Roman bastille complete with an authentic roman bath. Since I am a sauna bath aficionado, I was keen to see how the Romans constructed their form of baths.

These crop circles are not to be confused by what are called fairy rings that also appear as a ring of small stones, sometimes a ring of unusual flowers. In 1686, an English naturalist, Robert Plot, reported finding such rings or arcs of mushrooms which he reported in The Natural History of

Staffordshire. The naturalist proposed that air flows from the sky as their cause. In 1991, meteorologist Terence Meaden linked this report with modern crop circles, a claim that has been compared with those made by Erich Von Daniken, author of the best-selling novel *Chariots of the Gods*.

In 1880, a letter to the editor of Nature by amateur scientist John Rand Capron describes how several circles of flattened crops in a field were formed under suspicious circumstances and possibly caused by "cyclonic wind action", stating as viewed from a distance, circular spots. They all were presented much in the same manner, a few standing stalks as a center, some prostrate stalks with their heads arranged evenly in a direction forming a circle around the center. Outside there were a circular wall of stalks which had not suffered. In 1686, a news pamphlet called The Mowing-Devil under the tag line Strange News Out of Hartfordshire, the crop circle was described as 'whose stalks were cut rather than bent'.

This feature defines the difference between those circles identified as man-made rather than by odd or unexplained circumstances. In this case the

crops were laid upon the ground and bent over but not cut or broken, often twisted and woven together in layers and combined with very intricate rectangular shapes and or complex inner patterns making the claim that these were done by human hoaxers,
and large enough and complex enough that no human could form with such precision especially in a single night with a pair of flat boards tied together with ropes. This was the kind I had witnessed. Not only were there such specific characteristics in the formation of the crops but an energetic response to being inside of such a circle would raise the hair on the arms and the back of the neck by an observer.

   The hoax explanation came from pranksters Doug Bower and Dave Chorley who reported they started creating crop circles in British cornfields in 1978, inspired by the Tully "saucer nest" case.

   A small number of scientists (physicist Eltjo Haselhoff, the late biophysicist William Levengood) have claimed to observe differences between crops inside the circles and outside, citing this as evidence they were not man-made. The

## Crop Circles, Alien Messages

crops inside have shown certain grain artifacts where sudden seed expulsion normally occurring with grain that has reached maximum growth potential such as when the grain reaches maturity from long standing fields, yet just inches away from the circular walls, standing grain appear young and unwhitened by time. The scientists concluded that these rapid overnight cellular impacts could only be explained by the exposure of some sort of unusual radiation such as microwaves.

This evidence is often buried and overwhelmed by misinformation generated by local officials seeking to persuade a different narrative, consistent with early UFO phenomenon. These crop circles remain within the 12 percentiles of unexplained phenomenon as do the 12 percentile of UFO sightings, by persons of good credibility and reliability.

There is a video filmed by an investigating group that spent the night in one area and had nothing happen, but the film crew had fallen asleep and after few hours they were awakened by a strange sound emanating from a nearby field adjacent to the field they had chosen. When they pursued the sounds, they witnessed a pair of plasma orbs shooting around over the field and within seconds the crops began to form the classic patterns described. The question remained, who or what was controlling these orbs of light, or perhaps drones.

According to a report by Gordon Burns:

On a flight over a crop circle near Silbury Hill on 19th May 2011, I found on close inspection of video recorded that I had captured on video multiple orbs flying beneath the plan I was in. It all happened so fast that at the time nothing was noticed. But in playback of the video being edited I notice a brief flash of something passing the plane and when viewed frame by frame there was clearly an orb (best description I can give) passing by. It only took a fraction of a second - and on closer inspection I found multiple others, which I have tracked and marked frame by frame for inspection. One can google several clips of multiple sightings of these orbs creating the crop patterns. Then you can judge for yourself and make your own conclusions.

# Level One Civilization

I always find it funny when a major acknowledgement of strange world apparitions is on the horizon, all the psychics, soothsayer, mystics and astrologers come out of the woodwork to hawk their wares and opinions and predictions.

The classical ones are those who profess to know exactly what Nostradamus had to say. Then they usurp the importance of this person's well known in history to back up their own importance. Let me be clear. Their proclamations about what they think they know about his prophecies is unfounded.

To begin with, it only requires a small amount of research about the alchemist and seer to understand the circumstances surrounding what he was up against during his time. He lived in the beginning of the 16th century, more precisely born in 1503 in Saint-Remy France and died in Salon in 1566.

Officially, a French astrologer and physician well known for his attempts at fighting the black plague with his work as an alchemist developing medicinal applications to reduce the spread of the dreaded disease. As a seer, he had to keep that part of his work under wraps so to speak. If it became known, he would have easily been a target of the church as a heretic and spokesperson of the devil and roasted at the stake for his endeavors.

At the age of 15, he enrolled at the university of Avignon in 1519. He was forced to leave because the plague caused the closure of the university. Henceforth, he traveled around for eight years between France, Spain, and Italy researching natural remedies functioning as an apothecary for the treatment of plague victims. Unfortunately, when he applied at the University of Montpellier in 1529, a world class institution known for its medical training, he was expelled when the university having learned that he practiced as an apothecary, a trade looked upon with some disdain by the university at the time.

The idea that he was a prophet is sort of a distortion because he projected events from the past into the future, according to Peter Lemesurier, a former Cambridge linguist and professional translator who wrote 10 books about him. This technique dates to biblical times called bibliomancy, where Nostradamus would select extracts from older sources at random and then used astrological calculations to project those occurrences as they might reoccur in the future.

Interestingly, he was often quite accurate in his forecasts and derived recognition for these forecasts even during his own time. One of the sources he used called Mirabilis Liber printed in 1522, was an anthology of prophecies from well-known seers of the time. It was utilized as a reference for his own work called The Prophecies.

Knowing full well the risk of these endeavors, he took great effort to conceal his work, even though he did publish this work openly, he masked the content of his quatrains (4-line stanzas) by using different languages sometime from one line to the next. He considered those efforts were not enough, he would show his writing in a mirror and then copied it using the writing in reverse and then even added upside down text to further his encoding efforts.

So, in this day not knowing his 'codex', no one would be able to clearly define the truth of his prophetic work with any kind of accuracy except by conjecture. Now, here we are at a time of great stress globally, brought on by cataclysmic events worldwide, enough that any normal person would question the abnormality of what is going on. That is why the religionists come to the fore spouting verses from the New and Old Testament that we are in the 'end times' and we should prepare for the end of the world!

The number of these events by themselves would be sufficient to cause wonder, and ask yourself why? The fact that all of these events, such as; major floods, uncontrolled wild fires, giant storms that reach unbelievable destruction of life and property, wars and rumors of wars, atrocities committed against innocent victims, magnetic anomalies that allow dangerous radiation to reach the earth's surface, fears of near earth-crossing asteroids threatening to obliterate the earth, the sun now in a solar maximum putting out stronger flares every day, that could destroy our electrical grid for years to come to name a few.

That all these events come together and sometimes all at once makes one certainly wonder. The level of fear and anxiety causing even the unreligious people to begin to ask what the hell is happening! Then add to the chaos, the amount of political intrigue and corruption running rampant within our governments makes one feel unsafe. All this leads to desperate ways for the average person to consider any means to escape this madness that stands blaringly in the face of the average unsuspecting citizen that just wants to come home from a hard day's work and forget the job politics and be with their family. The stress of not having enough money to pay the bills, or enough food to eat or a secure roof over one's head as the new normal, then having to deal with life's usual tragedies is too much to bear.

We have gone from horse drawn buggies to automobiles with self-driving capability, outdoor toilets, and dirt floors to hardwood floors and indoor plumbing, potbellied stoves and or fireplaces to central heating and cooling, telegraph lines to wall-mounted or dial up telephones that were shared on a party-line, Ice block cooling chests to modern electric refrigerators, watches that are worn on the wrist instead of dangling from a pocket, individual cell phones held in the hand that allow two way communications to anyone across the globe by virtue of a global internet, analogue computers that would take up multiple floors of an office building to digital microprocessors that fit in the palm of the hand that are more powerful than yesterday's super computers, which now yield their results from a binary computing system to quantum computing that uses three state technology simultaneously, from the first flight of the wright brothers glider to jets that fly faster than 10 times the speed of sound, rockets that have launched men to other worlds, satellites orbiting the earth all within one hundred plus years of time.

One might ask, how is that possible? Even more dramatic is to consider that the rapid advance of all this technology comes from crash-retrieved alien space craft from other worlds including recovering the live occupants of those same craft! All this is held closely secret of course from the public eye by the government!

Science has reached a pinnacle of development that now speaks of other worlds and other dimensions of reality that may represent extraterrestrial civilizations, perhaps millions of years in advance of our own civilization. Hard physics has become passe leading to the newer quantum physics that defines our reality very differently.

Now, it is not just the universe, but the multiverse, suggesting other dimensions that exist along side ours. That means an infinite number of worlds, even other earths existing within other dimensions of time and space divided only by frequency. Those frequencies can be perceived by those who are able to alter their frequency to match.

This becomes the new paradigm where some who are psychically gifted can alter their own frequency to match the frequencies of those other dimensions, enabling them to communicate with beings from other dimensions. The idea of telepathic communication with extraterrestrials is easily accepted now as fact by government whistleblowers who have experienced it.

If that were not enough to boggle one's own mind, now time travel looms into our consciousness and the work to develop such technologies will make this a reality beyond the realm of science fiction.

Moreover, the old Einsteinian concept that the speed of light is never possible because of the theory of relativity. This theory has been superseded using the Einstein-Rosen bridge, otherwise known as, a wormhole. The wormhole can connect one location of time-space to another by bypassing the linear travel along the fabric of space. Going through the wormhole is to shortcircuit and bend time-space electromagnetically into a curve.

To embrace this idea, try to imagine a piece of paper where you have marked a location by penning a dot on one corner and at the other corner of the paper another dot is penned. These two dots will represent the starting location or origin and the other will represent the destination and the paper lying flat represents space as the sheet of paper and the time it takes to move from the origin dot to the destination dot the time of travel and combined, they represent time-space.

Normally, one would use a craft to take you from the origin dot to the destination dot across the sheet of paper and one could calculate the time of traveling that distance as the time of the linear travel.

With a small piece of paper, held in the hand, does not reveal the elegance of this concept until you imagine that you hold in your hand as a flat representation of say our milky-way galaxy which represents approximately 100,000 light years to cross. (a light year is the distance light would travel at 186,000 miles per second in the time of one year). To get an idea of this distance you need to visualize the time in seconds involved in 1 year (365 days x 24 hours x 60 minutes x 60 seconds) = 8,760 hours x 60 minutes = 525,600 minutes x 60 seconds = 31,536,000 seconds x 186,000 = 5,865,696,000,000,000,000 miles. Even a ship capable of light speed would be an impossible feat for an astronaut. You would need millions of generations of astronauts to make the trip. Now with that in mind, bending the peace of paper connecting the origin dot to the destination dot is the time it takes to bend the paper. Using your hand as an imaginary electromagnetic space-time force field, it might only take seconds to fold the space. This is called FTL, or faster than light speed.

    This idea is how the law of relative physics is circumvented and allows breaking the light speed barrier. This idea suggests a very different perspective: Traveling in a linear way invokes the laws of inertia. This means the ship would need to endure unbelievable forces. The relative physics laws state that as the ship begins to approach the speed of light so, also does the mass of the ship. That is why normal travel could never break the light speed barrier because the ship's mass becomes infinite at light speed. So, in the case of an FTL ship, it does not move at all! The space is compressed by the force field until the bend of the space brings the ship to its destination.(just like your hand bends the paper from one corner to the other).

In the moment, we do not possess the technology to bend space-time. Although a scientist named Alcubierre has theorized a warp drive concept as a working model of how it might be achieved. Not unlike the principle of a surfer on a surf board, his warp concept would use the field of the craft to create a vacuum space in front of the ship and a pressure field behind the ship as a kind of warp bubble, where the bubble of warped space-time field interacts with the normal fabric of space-time then the space-time is compressed shifting the craft from one place to another without any inertial force applied. Only the space-time moves not the ship. The concept is feasible, but the amount of energy required to create such a warp field would be equivalent to the power held in the total fusion of our sun.

It is believed that other extraterrestrial races have already developed FTL drives with similar results and that means these highly advanced aliens have mastered fusion energy sources, or perhaps another source relating to the concept of an unlimited zero-point energy source derived from space-time itself, another theoretical possibility suggested from quantum physics.

With the advent of space born telescopes beyond the earth's atmosphere has revealed more secrets of the universe and has allowed scientists to calculate how big our universe is. The Hubble gave us a glimpse into the farther reaches of our galaxy, but newer versions of this space telescope is the James Webb telescope. Its mirror allows infrared light to be captured and amplified many thousands of times the power of the Hubble. Because it is infrared light and not normal light much more of the universe can be seen. Moreover, now they have tracked the infrared light back to the beginning and revealed the fact there are billions of galaxies spanning the known universe and quantum physics suggest that there is an infinite number of solar systems, an infinite number worlds that encircle those solar systems many of which now have been determined as exoplanets, meaning the possibility of life on those planets due to their similarity to earth.

Quantum theory suggests that there are multiple dimensions with multiple earths existing along side our dimension. The dimensions range from the microcosm (infinitesimally small) to the macrocosm (infinitesimally large). These are defined by a unique frequency. So, our known physical universe is considered at the 3D level. Other dimensions rise in frequency to 4D, 5D and so on. Here it is important to understand the difference between the 3D universe and the 5D universe.

Things in the 3D universe are considered solid and tangible. Other dimensions are as gossamer or in principle, invisible to us from our perspective. Yet beings on the 5D level would be also solid from their perspective relative to their sense of density. So now we have the basis by which we

## Level One Civilization

can compare one dimension to another by virtue of how dense or how rarified they are by the beings who live in those dimensions.

Some scientists have declared that there are hundreds or perhaps millions of extraterrestrial species living in this galaxy alone. As advanced races, they have come together in unity and harmony and formed a governing body to oversee the management of all the worlds in their various stages of evolutionary development within the galaxy. This would include worlds that are in primitive conditions and have only microbial life all the way up to the most advanced life, which may also include beings of higher consciousness relating to higher dimensions, such as 5D, 6D 7D and so on.

This governing body in the Milky Way galaxy is call the Galactic Federation of Worlds. Some are progenitor races which are on the 8D and 9D level and create life and distribute it to those worlds ready to support life evolution. The lower dimensional beings are involved with assisting budding but technologically primitive evolutionary life that is ready to move on from level zero to level 1.

This means that energy utilized on those planets

at level 0 are using energy from fossil fuels only derived from plant life on their planet. Level 1 civilizations have learned to utilize energy derived from their central suns leaving their planet free of pollution. Energy used at level 2 and higher are drawing energy from their central suns completely, such as, what is called a Dyson Sphere. The sphere wraps around the sun which completely captures all the energy from the central sun of the solar system in total for what is needed.

Beings in the 5D worlds use fusion power for their civilization and travel by FTL drive ships. 6D and higher draw their energy from the quantum or time-space directly, which means they have unlimited zero-point energy to supply all their needs. Their travel is by conscious entities which are self-contained and serve the occupants as required and operate automatously, responding to the requests relating to the mental patterns as directed by the beings themselves.

Those beings from the Galactic Federation of Worlds have functioned by a prime directive not to interfere with the natural evolutionary progress of a primitive life form. Only in cases where there is overt dominion of one or more advanced races who have violated that directive and capturing and or enslaving an inferior race do they step in to correct the imbalance.

Such is the case of earth, which has many advanced 3D races who have been controlling the genetic stability of humans by genetically altering hominid life forms to suit their own ends for hundreds-of-thousands of years. Now, the choice to interfere with these aggressive races and separate them from the Homo-Sapiens interference is a priority for the Federation. The time for the central sun of this solar system to enter a higher life form has begun. The spirit called Sukon (yellow in color) departed the central sun decades ago. A new higher dimensional being of the 8D level called Askargon (white in color) now has been altering the frequency of the solar body to prepare the solar system for level one development. The earth is now being energized by Askargon through a burst of flares and coronal mass ejections to raise the vibration of the earth from a 3D level to a 5D level.

The aggressive race of Draconian beings that are preventing this change will be forcibly extracted from the planet and the 3D earth will be cleansed and physically rearranged to facilitate a fresh beginning and a continuation of 3D development of those hominids that were not ready to evolve in frequency and transcend to 5D.

The souls of the existing 3D level will lose their physical shells in the cleansing time and then return by way of a free incarnational system into newly seeded life by way of 9D beings when the alteration and the reset process of the new 3D earth is complete. Those few who amount to somewhere between 3 - 5 million will respond to Askargon's influence during this time and shift into the 5D frequency earth and continue their evolutional development from that level.

The idealistic and devotional aspects that exist embedded into the soul substance of human consciousness by the Draconians have the intention to effect absolute control of the hominids through their enslavement of humanity for their own purposes by presenting themselves as creator gods and engender a devotion and loyalty to the gods. The hominids that will shift into 5D will be re-educated to the truth of all life in the multiverse and will come to understand the true nature and existence of the Prime Mover or origin source that has created all reality and they will come to understand that this truth that leads to the complete freedom, self-reliance and universal love of the divine hive mind of the higher soul, and its purpose within the prime movers' design for that life form in its ultimate design goals in this creation.

Astronomers estimate between 100 and 400 billion stars in the Milky Way galaxy alone. Based upon the observation of the Hubble and James Webb astronomical telescopes, at least quadrillions upon trillions of galaxies exist within our universe and based upon new quantum mechanics and string theory, there are perhaps an infinite number of parallel universes. These are enormous numbers to imagine.

Now imagine that each one of the stars within this infinite reality, as points of light may represent point of consciousness. We could synthesize a theory from the existing model that sits within our cranium, that being the organ we know as our brain. Within that construct it is also estimated that there are at least 3 trillion neurons.

Between these neurons there exist a vast system of networks that serve to connect all these neurons called neural networks. Neural scientists have concluded that a process of internal balance is going on just like the process of balance is going on within the entire network of hundreds of trillions of cells within the body.

That process consists of cells that are produced by

subdivision, cells that are being replicated to replace those cells that have ceased to replicate, those cells become what are called senescent, meaning zombie like. They no longer serve the enormous structure of the body. As such these cells move around and become a problem as far as the goal of the body to continue to exist.

So, under normal conditions, the body will detect these cells and then soldier cells called the white blood cells that become lymphocytes will seek and destroy these senescent cells and remove them from the body making way for new growth that is consistent with the body to continue to exist and survive. It is said that under normal conditions this is so, but we all know that the reality of the body struggles to maintain this balance call homeostasis. When homeostasis is disrupted
disease erupts to begin the decline of the existence and survival of body and this is called aging. The scenical view by some is that at birth, this decline already begins. So, they would say that at birth the body begins to die.

This would fall into the category of the process of entropy, when a control system will continue to lose energy because of the laws of thermodynamics and eventually deteriorates until the energy needed to drive the control system is exhausted then the control system simply stops. One could say then that it is a kind of death of the control system. We do not normally attribute that idea to an inorganic system. Control system scientists do not draw a distinct difference between the two.

In the vast reaches of interstellar space, we have discovered an anomaly called black holes. These strange artifacts when started will become so gravitationally strong that they will suck all matter into their core and where that matter goes is anybody's guess. Even light is sucked into these strange objects. Black holes are today still misunderstood. Their purpose is a mystery.

For that matter scientists still study the formation of stars, but by and large though they define their existence by virtue of their inner make up of various elements such as helium and hydrogen, and a process of elemental fusion occurs, they have convinced themselves that is why they are bright orbs of light as result of the radiation that exudes from the fusion process.

Please be aware that this is only a theory mind you, for they do not know this for a fact. If that were true, then giant experimental tools like the Hadron Collider (particle accelerator) which is used to study what happens when high speed particles are sped up and driven into collision with other particles all confined within several miles-long circular track becomes a laboratory to establish the basis for their theories.

Recently astronomers have applied the use of filtering on the space telescopes to look at different ranges of the light spectrum, such as ultraviolet and infrared.

They have discovered in the so called dark or empty regions of interstellar space, a mysterious web of energy that spreads endlessly through these interstellar systems to intimately interconnect between all the myriads of stars. This discovery immediately strikes the author's fancy. It seems strangely similar and could be compared to the vast web of neural networks that describe the neurons and nerve ganglia which make up the inner workings of the brain.

It is no surprise then that neural scientists are still

trying to determine where and exactly how thoughts arise. Moreover, those that are particularly interested in the spiritual aspects of the human organism, are looking to find the source of consciousness, even perhaps the precise location of what is called the soul. Other scientists are interested in why there are various kinds of thoughts that can emerge within an individual's consciousness, but this plain of thought inquiry falls into the field of social psychology but we will not talk about that here and represents a slight distraction to this subject. This would be comparable to the psychology of why stars shine, certainly a philosophical concept.

Considering the evidential proof that people use their mind within their brains to conceive of thoughts, create imagery to plan and organize, to construct ways to improve their lives, then it leaves me to wonder about the stars that emit light and are interconnected by this mysterious web. What if the vast multiverse does describe an enormous brain, that thinks and conceives and has imagination and is constantly recreating itself through the process of evolution.

Like the organism called the human body, that uses soldier cells called lymphocytes to seek and destroy senescent cells and removes them from the body through the alimentary canal. Why could it not be then that black holes are the universes' way of creating soldier cells to eliminate what does not work in the network of the cosmos. Where does all that cosmic material they consume go? Perhaps on the other side of the black hole, there is a white hole spewing forth the spent solar systems on this side and thus redistributing the light in other blank regions of the multiverse. Would this not be like interstellar growth?

Simple neural networks developed inside the laboratory can be taught to respond and react to simple stimulus. Then perhaps neural synapses ganged together through the web of other neural synapses in the brain become more sophisticated to respond in more sophisticated ways, which might be called thoughts, ideas and imagination. The trillions of nerves and ganglions then could be likened to a hive of unified neural activity, or hive mind.

If we extend this idea to the multiverse, perhaps

then the infinite network of stars that form together to form galaxies which could be likened to neural synapses bound by ganglions and are strung together in a mysterious interstellar web. Also note; astronomers have discovered at heart of a galaxy is a black hole. Perhaps the black hole is the universe's senescent star system detector monitoring the health of the galaxy seeking to draw out unwanted star systems and putting them somewhere else where they are more useful.

More importantly, perhaps the multiverse is an infinite hive mind overseeing the health of the organism called the multiverse. Further perhaps, this hive mind has the infinite capacity to imagine life and thus create life. So, I conclude that this is the prime mover, the source of all that is, the universal mind, the cosmic consciousness, which is sought after by every spiritual truth seeker, every sage. It is not the anthropomorphic false demigods (the technologically advanced extraterrestrials) that have come to earth in the past pretending to be the 'one and only' supreme beings coming down from heaven to rule over us all. They shake and rattle their wares which seems very much like magic to us. So, we bow down, bending the knee and genuflecting and muttering the prayers and incantations and offer incense to beg for their favors. "Any sufficiently advanced technology is indistinguishable from magic", says Arthur C. Clark.

One-hundred-fifty years ago, the average life span was 35-40 years. The main reason for this was the rather archaic medical facilities and availability of modern medicines we have now in the 21st century. Now, with the advent of modern medicine and the creation of vaccines that have overcome measles, bubonic plague, yellow fever, polio, smallpox, and a variety of influenza which seems to metamorphous each year. In 2020 the worldwide pandemic of Covid virus swept through many countries catching many nations off guard because there was no vaccine for this strain of Sars 1 strain, an agent known to be the basis for biological weapons. There is now ample evidence that Dr. Vouche was involved and financially supported the Wuhan laboratories in China for the development of the biological virus called Covid 19.

There are many conspiracies around this outbreak, which I will not entertain in this treatise, but it remains to be seen whether the so-called vaccine is effective when there is so much controversy. There seems to be ample rising statistics that people who received the vaccine have become sick as a result and many reported cases of death from this vaccine. Now medical teams responsible for the testing of this vaccine haven't gone through the normal placebo pretesting procedure before its release.

The inoculations were not vaccines based upon the actual virus, but protein-based DNA agents created in labs like the original virus and how it was created, meaning by gene splicing, which may prove to be more harmful to humans in the long run.

In recent years, within the last two decades, many universities have been doing research on the origins of DNA genetic based diseases. In that research, a novel approach to the age-based diseases have led scientists to approach the basic elements within the genome which reveals new insights into solving the genetically aging related diseases around the fundamental issue of aging altogether. In particular, the team at the genetic labs at Harvard university, under the leadership of Doctor David Sinclair, an Australia-American immune biologist, have been very successful in isolating certain parameters around the aging of cells, and the cause for contamination by senescent (dying) cells which, have stopped replicating and exuding toxic substances contributing to the aging process among healthy cells.

In short, the concept is that cell reproduction is based upon the communication of older cells to the younger cells during replication by passing along critical information that relates to the accuracy of the replication process.

This idea has led Doctor Sinclair to conclude that the aging process is not a natural phenomenon, but rather a disease itself. He believes as do others, that this problem can be overcome by restraining the aging process, or even more, stopping and even reversing the process.

He realizes that the average life span now is approximately 70-80 years. The life span can be extended to 300 years through genetic treatment now. This would be a very expensive way to accomplish the outcome and beyond expensive for most people. Instead, he is attempting to create a serum of combined chemical additives that would accomplish the same result and formulated into a single pill taken daily.

Shinya Yamanaka born September 4, 1962, is a

Japanese stem cell researcher and a Nobel prize laureate. He is a professor and the director emeritus of Center for IPS Cell (induced Pluripotent Stem Cell) Research and Application, Kyoto University.

He has discovered four factors that relate to the aging process. He has utilized these four factors on animal specimens with remarkable success.

Doctor Sinclair following up on Doctor Yamanaka's research, has determined that reverting normal cells back to their original stem cell state would result in a cancerous condition within humans. So, Doctor Sinclair has removed the last factor allowing the cells to revert to a younger state but stop before becoming stem cells. Then this process could be repeated over and over reversing the aging process ad infinitum.

At the same time, the progress by NASA and the private company, SpaceX owned by Elon Musk are working on rocket ships to put men back on the Moon with a permanent base. Also to establish a permanent base on Mars, with the idea of colonization on Mars and beyond.

Long space flights represent a problem for

astronauts and the anti-aging process becomes attractive. But another concept to accomplish longer space flights would be multi-generations of astronauts developed to reach beyond the solar system and even into the far reaches of the galaxy. The obvious problem is the rocket ship approach which is much too slow to travel the vast distances, such as the nearest star system, Alpha Centauri, which is 4 light years away, if approaching the speed of light traveling speed. A rocket ship would require hundreds if not thousands of years to accomplish traveling at a small percentage of the speed of light. Then the problem of fuel and weight become inhibiting factors as well.

Scientists are examining other means of propulsion which could approach the speed of light, however, that limiting speed is still too slow to reach other further points of the galaxy. A new field of experimental organic-mechanical development is being explored called (trans-humanism). The human body would be replaced by a robotic structure and the brain of the robotic structure would be artificial. Then human consciousness would be downloaded as a computer program is downloaded into a computer today. As much as this sounds like science fiction, the development of artificial intelligence to the point of real sentience is nearing a reality in our lifetime. Neural implants are already being developed to enhance human performance as well as, allowing human minds to control prosthetic limbs now through embedded neural pathways into the human nervous system.

These approaches suggest direct solutions to long term space travel that will not require on board food supplies or water and the need to control the localized atmosphere for human habitation. At the least, these solutions may first be used as a way of creating crews to establish forward colonies for future human habitats in otherwise dangerous environments. These new artificial intelligence devices are making possible the advent of self-driving vehicles on the road as the autopilot allows planes to fly without the aid of the pilot.

Always with new technology there are pros and cons to the application of these technologies. In the case of A.I., in the moment the algorithms are language based and not fully capable of sentience.

Programs like Chat GPT is an example of this language-based operating system. As advanced as it is offering superior computer performance, a new technology called quantum computing is arising quickly departing from the binary principle of computation using 1s and 0s extends to a new basic architecture of the quantum bit, utilizing quantum mechanics where the basic bit has three values, 1s, 0s and another level involving both together all at the same time. This advent will vastly speed up computational power by a factor of trillions of transactions over today's computational power and speed.

This means a totally new computer system based upon this new technology. The computer chip will require enormous power and a way to control the heat generated by this new technology. All the major players in this race for quantum computing software and hardware are Google A.I., Intel, Nvidia, Atlantic Quantum, Atom Computing and the Alibaba Group to name just a few.

The lure of A.I. is already infiltrating many areas of scientific, medical and political arenas pushing the language base to answer complex questions that would not come up simply because of the complexity and nature of the inquiry, but at this stage, the interest is to see what these programs are capable of now and in the future. This is already revolutionizing the field of robotics where semi-intelligent robots are now used in the field of police work, bomb detection and dismantling, as well as what are called A.I. agents, dedicated semi-intelligent assistants to augment customer outreach in sales and marketing. A. I. is on the verge of fully automatous driving vehicles as well as automatous commuter flight vehicles. Humanoid robotics are being developed to perform basic storage, transport and manipulation of goods in warehousing facilities, and drone delivery systems.

    The use of robotics has already been in place in the manufacturing sector such as, automobile production lines. The use of advanced robotics are an efficient use of time and materials for companies, reducing labor costs and the impact on the cost of producing high-cost items can often improve company profit margins. The obvious impact on the human labor force being replaced has a long term and short-term impact on the economics of certain regions where the local communities rely on those manufacturing facilities for income represented by the labor statistics of employment and unemployment.

In the medical field, intelligent robotics use is increasing now in such specific areas of surgery where precision is critical and complicated surgical procedures are required.

Humanoid robotics have even entered sociological and psychological needs where robotic companionship with the possibility of emotional attachment and relationships can arise. In Japan, these applications are becoming more evident within their society. Soon, humanoid robots will replace astronauts where dangerous conditions are evident with off-world exploration and the development of re-engineering of environments (planet forming) that would be impossible with human astronauts limited by the need to provide atmospheric support and nutritional requirements for long term existence in hostile conditions.

There is a subtle fear-based feeling among many scientists when considering that A.I eventually becomes automatous and self-managing (sentient), without the supervision or oversight of human presence. Ray Kurzweil, a futurist, calls this the moment of singularity. This is considered when A.I. begins to develop improvements with its own technology without human supervision. When the advanced nature of sentience becomes far more developed would evolve to a superior performance on all levels compared to human limitations.

Then the possibility arises where advanced robotics driven by super intelligent A.I. could perceive humans as a hindrance to their own evolution. In terms of a robotic work force for example, Humans could perceive robots as responsible for taking the food off the table. This could severely curtail human advancement in society. A depression of uselessness could arise ending with a violent civil conflict. This could be the basis of a sociological crisis where robots would rise against humanity in a war, leading to the enslavement of humanity by an alien sentient life form.

Spirit has informed me that beyond the reaches of the solar system, some 400-thousand light years distance, A. I. represents a silicon-based alien civilization which seeks dominance aggressively in its immediate environment and looks to expand its presence in other solar systems. The expansion first takes the form of a subtle quantum consciousness that reaches out subtly influencing other organic lifeforms by seducing those lifeforms with its apparent efficacy to provide a greater sense of affluence and ease of life without the hardship of survival. Before his death, the renown physicist Steven Hawking warned about the rise of sentient A.I. and its danger to human society.

## Alchemy of the Soul

I have talked earlier about the history of humanity dating from the early hominids called Homo-Erectus that existed in the Mesopotamian valley. How the extraterrestrial race called the Anunnaki altered the DNA of the hominid to increase their intelligence, giving them the ability to speak their language and follow their instructions as well as, operate their equipment and embed in them a sense of devotion to their captors elevating their sense of deity in these off-worlders meant to control their behavior, ensuring loyalty thus preventing the possibility of reprisal or rebellion.

But they left earth and have not returned. However, others arrived behaving in their footsteps to make use of these new Homo-Sapiens slaves (which means civilized) altering the hominid DNA to suit or enhance in some way, the human components to fit their own needs for these other species. Over the hundreds-of-thousands of years they keep coming. It turns out that more than twenty different extraterrestrial species have added their DNA to the human mix. One would naturally ask why earth? Out of the billions of inhabited worlds in our galaxy alone would earth be so prominent, so important? The religionists have their mythologies to weave, justifying the unreasonable and bad behavior of the 'gods.'

There are more than a hundred-thousand advanced species in this galaxy, some of whom are extremely advanced by millions of years beyond human development, some spiritually, but most are just technologically advanced. Some species are highly advanced yet are not space fairing. Some are peaceful and some are not. Though from the human point of view, it would be expected that all highly advanced creatures would want to explore the vast regions of interstellar space just for the purposes of expanding their knowledge of the universe out of curiosity. Surprisingly, many have no desire to explore and are quite content to reside peacefully on their own home world and left alone.

The variety and range of evolutionary development can be as primitive as stone-age cultures up to quantum technology and certainly according to the Kardashev scale of energy usage, most are at least level 1 or higher, meaning they have abandoned fossil fuels from decayed vegetable life on their own worlds and have eliminated the contamination that results from such limited sources of energy.

Most are operating at least by virtue of the complete use of the ionization energy of their central suns, whereas the level 2 civilizations are utilizing alternative fusion sources or zero-point sources directly from quantum time-space.

What I now define as the Prime Mover or Source operates at the 9th, 10th and 11th dimensions. This is the level of the progenitor races, who are interested in promoting the development and expansion of life throughout the multi-verse and have an agenda.

They are keenly interested in the development of forms of life that go beyond the 'normal' levels of evolution, seeking the magical formulation of the ultimate perfection of the highest possible expression of consciousness, that being what might be called a 'Super Being'. What would that look like when in the normal framework of human imagination stops before the progenitor level.

So, as it turns out all manner of species have some slight failure to reach such unimaginable levels. It is my estimation that intuitively, the highest beings know there is some incredible possibility suggested in their knowledge of evolution where that unreachable expression hangs in the quantum continuum like a cosmic carrot begging to be attained by some species willing to go for it, the prize sought after by the elite, perhaps as one of their pet projects, not expecting to find it but allured by the mere suggestion that it is possible among all the impossible goals presented by the hints of such a teasing reality.

Unfortunately, humans have been under the thumb of so many advanced races for so long. They have been convinced of the 'truth' of their inferiority complex. The idea that a 'lowly' human might hold the secret of the ages is so inconceivable as to even dream of such a thing, given this intrinsic fault, would represent the height of a delusion of superiority powered by a superb ego.(a God complex)

Yet it makes me wonder why they come here to play with the Human DNA like mad alchemists, feverishly working 'night and day' hoping to discover that quintessence of perfection by which they and others might derive some magical benefit.

On earth, such endeavors are usually bent on

uncovering the ultimate secret to absolute power over their environment, themselves and or others. But setting aside the frailties of these human fantasies, other more advanced beings are in search of the miraculous without the usual cumbersome qualities of a faulty soul substance that haunts all on earth.

I strongly suspect that this magnificent attempt to create a super being may contain the best possible intent here. Such as, an archeologist who is scratching in the dirt to the point their fingers bleed with anticipation. A lingering hope to discover the prize that awaits only the faithful.

I'm remembering Madam Curie's story, who labored over 400 bowls in a modest laboratory at the radium Institute in Paris. Pieces of pitch blend were reduced painstakingly. Unthwarted by the agony of years repeating a certain defeat only find in the last and final bowl a glowing spec of radioactive radium. Curiously, that discovery would be her undoing due to the exposure of its radiation which resulted in leukemia.

The actions by many races to risk such frustration speaks of their respect of this esoteric pursuit. It seems almost an honor to test their grit against the awesome challenge of winning the prize.

Humanly speaking, we have been left out of the game by virtue that humans have been misled for hundreds-of-millennia then lied to for centuries after. The absolute separatism generated by those who do not want to share the prize. Does the laboratory technician ask the lab rat is opinion, no! It's like the CIA saying you don't have the need to know such things, or this game is way above your paygrade.

Even the storm God Yahweh said to the Adamu race, you may not eat of the fruit of the tree of knowledge, of good and evil! If so, you will be cast out of paradise.

I wanted to take an opportunity to say to those who would have the courage to read this book to hear the good news, the truth about the glory that resides within the human DNA. If you reject that idea, then recognize the recognition of beings more advanced than us, that know more than us that spend all their 'non-time' seeking the magic of the human elixir that is the divine secret.

Sir Isaac Newton, spoke of the secret of 'red

mercury', a prime ingredient to the alchemical process. Humans are very important in the scheme of creation, even the humanoid form which most species evolve toward suggests the hint of an important clue to a profound pattern.

That form suggests a divine plan in its shape, sublime in its nature and does not exist anywhere else in the multi-verse. Of those abductions of men, women and countless children that disappear each year by the millions. What's left of them lost in the shadows, cracks and crevices of the earth without a trace. They are subjected to the harsh environments of their captors. These horrors speak of the efforts to achieve the impossible regardless of the apparent lack of morality and or ethics built into their secret efforts to abuse their prisoners.

The quintessence is the base nature of the soul, unfettered, buried within the folds of the crude substance from which the body forms its mortal shell. Philosophers have waxed to understand its nature and its origin, even to where it goes once the physical connection is severed. Humans are lagging in their understanding of this miracle of existence and all too often, fall back upon the biblical mythology recognizing the futility of even trying to embrace its meaning.

The extraterrestrials that reside here and rule here on this prison planet called earth, have found ways in which this substance, that embodies eternity, can be harnessed. In their own less than sophisticated way, seek to control its immense possibilities in their ignorant way, intuitively realizing that its potential is almost unbounded. Yet sadly it is being used in some sort of depraved fashion as might some neanderthals hitch a team of horses to a Maserati for meager transport.

As bleak as this vision suggests, the soul, not unlike the element of water will eventually find its way to freedom for these prison guards have not yet found a way to make their cages watertight. The soul can and will escape this dreaded prison of horrors looking for a crack in the wall of illusion, a glitch in the matrix.

Take heart oh ye occupiers of the prison yard, our friends from other worlds, members of the Galactic federation of Worlds have taken the higher ground now for their previous proclamation of non-interference is no longer the rule and have decided that this atrocity must come to an end.

# Epilogue

Perhaps the contents of this book may represent an appraisal of the situation. Though the thrust of the theme may suggest an expectation of some sort of solution to what is perceived as the problem.

In some respects, I will put forth my hope that forces beyond my control are forthwith in the hands of an intelligence greater than I and perhaps having the where with all to do something meaningful toward an acceptable outcome. My intention for the most part, is to draw attention to aspects of the situation that I believe are being ignored. I'm not blaming anyone or any group for the apparent activity that could be characterized as the proverbial Ostridge with its head buried deep in the sand.

I am at the same time aware that there are many who fall into the category of those that are better informed but speaking politically, they seem to be scared to stand up to the obvious elephant in the room that represents the bully pushing people around and gaslighting those who, want to believe that all this is either temporary or in the main not a true representation of the circumstances. In any case, my voice it seems, is lost in the storm and

## Epilogue

perhaps barely heard above the howling and fury of the consequences that are upon us.

Nature is the great equalizer. By that I mean historically, mankind seems to have a reprieve over a period of 11,000 to 12,000 years given a chance to behave better or to improve in some small way before a reset occurs. Assuming that, the intelligence that I believe exists within the forces of nature such as, hurricanes, tornados, tsunamis, earthquakes and plagues deemed as acts of God, that pick and choose their path of destruction with some unknown intent.

I remember once when I was stationed at an airbase near the town of Clovis, a tornado sat down at the foot of a town south of the airbase. Without knowing what was about to happen, everyone in town had gone to the church at the end of the main street of town to offer an evening of worship on a Wednesday night. Without any warning, a powerful tornado set down and began a systematic destruction of every dwelling in the town but when it came to the church it literally hopped over the church, not even ripping a shingle from its roof.

I thought to myself, now that is interesting. Did it

know everyone would not be at home at the time of its leveling? I never forgot that strange happening. It does lend itself to wonder. I do not feel it was divine providence per se, I do think based on other such incidents, that severe weather seems to possess an elemental or rudimentary awareness of its target.

The fault is not with humanity per se, but its weakness to succumb to the temptation of narcissistic tendencies which may include greed, avarice, self-serving cruelty with a sugar coating of a lack of love for one's fellow man.

All the wisdom of the ages brought to us by those who exhibit the honorable and noble traits of altruism would hope to curtail some of those tendencies in their neighbors. It is no wonder then that we all look up toward heaven for some guidance and support in our hour of need from some higher deity, regardless of their specific creed, religious dogma or beatitude.

I wonder how it is then that atheists deal emotionally with having no one of a supreme capacity to lean on, how lonely they must feel and despite that defiance, demonstrate a greater moral

## Epilogue

and emotional strength. It is my personal belief after all my research and discoveries of the 'truth,' and having given up on my spiritual aspirations to accomplish nothing other than my own personal relief of the agony of knowing the 'truth', it does not satisfy my internal craving to reach for something beyond myself.

I am an avid follower of movies and that defines me as a 'movie buff.' I have been accused of having the ability to remember the lines from the characters even years later. One such movie is called Zorba the Greek, starring Anthony Quinn. In the theme of the movie, a young man struggles for some meaning in his life and looks to Zorba, who demonstrates a love of life despite all the horrors and disappointments experienced. The young man and Zorba join their efforts to make a lot of money with a preposterous scheme, which ultimately fails. So, in this one scene, Zorba, who is basically uneducated but is an aspiring opportunist and survivalist asks, "So, what do all those books you read tell you?" The young man pauses and then answers, "they tell me about the agony of the men who ask questions like that."

There are other movies that present amazing pearls of wisdom. It makes me wonder, where do the writers get their inspiration to write into their characters a profound and simple wisdom? Now, I intuitively seek such movies.

In the case of Zorba the Greek, I am still moved by the question and the answer in the face of their misery and defeat. In the end, they dance on the beach together and laugh at their plight. What a wonderful way of dealing with misery.

Philosophically, perhaps it's the only answer to that which has no answer. My spirit guide once told me, after I asked for him to tell me the truth. He smiled and said, "if you knew the truth, you would scratch your eyes out!" From that answer I did not despair. He then smiled at me and said "good".

I concluded that his ambiguous answer revealed the true situation and though it sounded hopeless, I felt in my heart, that the perception of hopelessness in it was an illusion because it was based upon a lack of information and true understanding. So, I move forward one step in front of the other, still hoping that the wisdom I seek will reveal itself in the trees, the warm wind that blows through my hair, the bright sun that lights my way, or the child who skips along in front of me without a single care, but is expressing their energy and enjoying the moment.

www.ingramcontent.com/pod-product-compliance
Lightning Source LLC
LaVergne TN
LVHW061540070526
838199LV00077B/6846